A Pocket Guide to the Bible

Kevin O'Donnell

Published by
Lion Hudson plc
Mayfield House, 256 Banbury Road,
Oxford OX2 7DH, England
www.lionhudson.com
ISBN 0 7459 5131 7

First edition 2004
10 9 8 7 6 5 4 3 2 1 0

Acknowledgments

Scripture quotations taken from the Holy Bible,
New International Version, copyright © 1973, 1978, 1984
International Bible Society. Used by permission of Zondervan
and Hodder & Stoughton Limited. All rights reserved.
The 'NIV' and 'New International Version' trademarks
are registered in the United States Patent and Trademark
Office by International Bible Society. Use of either trademark
requires the permission of International Bible Society. UK
trademark number 1448790.

A catalogue record for this book is available
from the British Library

Typeset in 8.5/12 Garamond ITC Lt BT
Printed and bound in Malta

Contents

Getting to Know the Bible

The Bible is a bit like the works of Shakespeare. Everyone knows of it, and it's always one of the things that is suggested that you might have with you on a desert island. The idea seems to be that you would have plenty of the time necessary to give it the attention that is its due as one of humankind's classic literary accomplishments, and, quite honestly, most of us have the nagging sense that, even if we consider ourselves to be educated people, we don't really know either the Bible or Shakespeare as well as we should. Fortunately for Shakespeare, however, the educational system usually gives us some exposure to him. Only passing glimpses of the Bible might have been engaged with during school life, though, and was anybody really listening?

Not a Novel

The Bible is not to be read from cover to cover like a novel. It doesn't work like Jane Austen or Jackie Collins. If you've ever tried, you've probably ground to a halt somewhere in Exodus (the second book of the Old Testament) with all the long lists of laws. The word 'Bible' is from a Greek word meaning 'books'. The Bible is a collection of 66 books that were written by different people at different times. If you went back in time, say before the start of the 1st century AD, a Bible would have filled a whole shelf or a huge box, for the books would have been on separate scrolls, rolled up. The book format that we know today was invented about the time of Jesus.

The books are different styles of literature, too; there are stories, historical lists, genealogies, law codes, poems, hymns and a powerful style called prophecy. The writings are not only spiritual thoughts and moral guidance; there are all sorts of things in there. It is not a book (or books) of pure enlightenment with lists of wise sayings by someone like a Zen master. We need a guide to find our way through the Bible, such as a handbook to the Bible, or a commentary on a particular book, that will provide all sorts of background information. This little book is to slip into your pocket to dip into as you wish. It gives a brief synopsis of the major features and stories of each book of the Bible, and a few key things to think about.

In Two Parts

The first thing to grasp about Bible reading is that the Bible falls into two sections, a Part One and a Part Two – what Christians refer to as the Old and New Testaments. Christians believe that Part One is a preparation for Jesus, and Part Two is about him and what happened after he came. That preparation took over a thousand years and traces the development of the faith of the Hebrews from very early and primitive beginnings until they had more sublime and enlightened thoughts about God and how we should treat one another. (The New Testament, in contrast, was put together over about 70 years!) The long preparation goes some way to explain why there are some things in there that seem to be odd or even cruel in the early parts of the Scriptures. It is a bit like in Arthur C. Clarke's *2001, A Space Odyssey*, where an advanced alien race communicates with developing humans in stages, imparting knowledge little by little until they are ready to handle it. There is a progressive revelation, a gradual unveiling of what God is really like. Christians believe that what we see in the life of Jesus is what God really is about, though much light shines in the Old Testament writings, too – particularly in the great prophets and later writings.

There is a sense, too, among Christians, that in the earlier days God was working from a different angle, sometimes almost at arm's length. This was pre-Jesus, and before his death on the cross that allowed people to know forgiveness and to draw near. The Hebrews had all sorts of sacrifices to help them cover up their sins temporarily. There are mercy and compassion expressed in the Old Testament, but they come to perfect fruition in Jesus.

Testaments and Covenants

The terms 'Old Testament' and 'New Testament' need some translating. A 'testament' suggests a solemn oath, a written pledge that something will be so, like a 'Last Will and Testament'.

The term is a translation of Hebrew and Greek words that also can mean 'covenant'. This, in the ancient world, was a binding agreement between two parties, often involving the ritual slaughter of animals to seal it in blood. Moses instituted the old covenant with its animal sacrifices and altars, as well as the moral code that God expected his people to follow, the Ten Commandments. But there was an older covenant recorded in the Bible, one with Abraham, an ancestor of Moses. Abraham's covenant was one of promise – all the nations would be blessed through his offspring. Christians believe that this promise was fulfilled in Jesus, the promised messiah, and the old ritual of Moses was brought to an end.

'Messiah' is a word that means 'anointed one' or 'chosen one'. It was used for the Israelite kings, who were anointed with holy oil and blessed by God. However, the Old Testament looked forward to the coming of a special, holy king, and Christians believe that this king was Jesus of Nazareth. Jesus brought a new covenant, sealed with his own blood shed upon the cross. He shows us that God is bound to his creation, to you and to me, for all time, by having become one of us and having suffered for us.

Looking for Jesus in the Old Testament

If the Hebrew Scriptures of the Old Testament were a preparation for Jesus, then there should be all sorts of hints and clues about his coming in them. Many think that there are, though some are rather indirect and can only be applied to him with hindsight.

Each section of the Old Testament has something about Jesus in it – a verse, image or idea that Christians have seen as being fulfilled by him or as prefiguring him. Jesus set the precedent for this, himself: after rising from the dead, he walked with two disciples to Emmaus. In conversation, he opened the Scriptures to them and taught them how so many spoke of him, from Moses to the prophets (see Luke 24:25–32).

Some Old Testament passages are seen as directly predicting Jesus, such as Isaiah 7:14 about a virgin conceiving. Others are more indirect, being symbols and details that can be given a Christian meaning. Thus, a woman hangs a red cord from her window to show that her house is safe from attack (Joshua 2:17–21). The red suggests the blood of Christ and the salvation that comes from him. These symbols are known as types of Christ, not direct prophecies but indirect hints and associations with him and the work of God the Father through him.

In some books of the Old Testament there are no particular prophecies or types. Instead, there are general themes or ideas that Christians believe were summed up in Jesus, such as the righteous and faithful teacher of the Law.

In summary, there are three levels of speaking about Jesus in the Hebrew Bible:

- ❑ Direct prophecies
- ❑ Types (symbols that can be linked to Jesus)
- ❑ General themes that were fulfilled in his life completely.

Inspired?

Christians speak of the Bible as being 'inspired' or as 'the Word of God'. There are many different interpretations of this – some see certain Bible passages, such as the creation stories, as symbolic, and some see them as literal. Some argue that there are no faults at all in the Scriptures, even in things to do with geography or history or science. Others would hold this idea of inerrancy only for spiritual matters. In this book we shall generally pass over these debates, as well as difficulties with the interpretation of some passages, and what archaeology might or might not show at times. For a deeper study, consult the bigger handbooks or commentaries.

What Do We Make of Miracles?

There are a number of miracle stories or amazing events in the Bible, whether things like healings or the Red Sea waters parting. People have different ideas about and interpretations of these, ranging from a full-blown belief in divine, supernatural intervention, to God working through natural events and forces that were not understood then. (For more information, please see the appendix at the end of the book.) What all can agree upon is that when the presence of God is involved, all sorts of forces might come into play to bring blessing.

On a Personal Level

What we can say is that God speaks through the pages of the

Bible – that, however he does it, his Word comes alive and hits our hearts. There is something very sacred and special about the collection, or canon, of books that the early church accepted as being divinely inspired. Despite difficulties with some passages, the collection is sacramental – human words convey a spiritual blessing. The only way to find this out is to experience it; read prayerfully and bathe in God's Word. The apostle Paul even spoke of being washed by the Word (Ephesians 5:26), and there is a sense of peace, of refreshing, of guidance and of even changing the patterns of how we think about some issues (what, in Bible-speak, is called 'the renewing of the mind'). Nowadays we look for all sorts of alternative therapies to help us focus and relax – but what better way than devotional reading of the Bible? The Scriptures contain something alive and active. As the author of the Epistle to the Hebrews put it:

> 'For the word of God is living and active. Sharper than any double-edged sword, it penetrates even to dividing soul and spirit, joints and marrow; it judges the thoughts and attitudes of the heart.'
>
> **Hebrews 4:12**

How to Use this Book

Either use this little book as a sampler of the Bible or as a way to devotedly and consistently work through it. Dip into a section here and there and use the guidance notes, or, if you prefer, start at Genesis and work through, week by week, until you reach Revelation. Using this book won't make you a biblical expert overnight, but it will give you a clear overview. You will end up with a broad picture that, I hope, you will find useful and enlightening.

Introduction to the Law

The books of Moses, the first five books of the Old Testament, are known as the Torah – the 'Law' or the 'Way'. For Jews, it was and still is a divine Highway Code through life. These are the most sacred books of the Hebrew Scriptures, and synagogues have them written out on traditional scrolls. These are brought out of a central container and carried about in a procession with great reverence.

There are a number of questions and points to consider before plunging into each book. The five books are Genesis, Exodus, Leviticus, Numbers and Deuteronomy. Genesis is full of stories of creation and early ancestors and is not really about laws and commandments. These are to be found in the other four books of the Torah, and they number, according to traditional Jewish scholarship, 613 commandments in total. Some are ethical (dealing with behaviour between people or in society) and some are ritual commandments. There are stories about Moses and the early Hebrews in these other four books, but there are often long collections of laws. They are more like reference books.

Olden Days?

Some of the old laws seem antiquated, dealing with early farming community issues such as oxen that wander into a neighbour's fields. Many of the ritual laws concern what to eat or not to eat, such as pork or shellfish. Others are concerned with the type of sacrifice that should be offered at different festivals or to atone for various sins; who should eat the flesh of the animal, if anyone at all; what should be done with the fat; and where one should put the blood. However, the ethical commandments still resonate today, such as the Ten Commandments or the command to 'love your neighbour as yourself' (see Exodus 20:1–17 and Leviticus 19:9–18), cited by Jesus as one of the two most important of all the laws.

What Do We Make of the Old Laws?

In modern times, the Jewish community debates what sense to make of the old laws. More liberal Jews think some laws are antiquated and can be relaxed, while more traditional Jews take them all as divine and eternal. The church teaches that Jesus set aside the ritual laws, but the ethical ones are still binding. The idea is that the Torah was a preparation for Christ, a pointer, offering rituals and practices that taught people about the reality of sin, the costliness of forgiveness and the need to approach God in holiness. The apostle Paul described the Torah as a 'schoolmaster' preparing the way of Christ (Galatians 3:24–25). The writer of Hebrews says:

'The law is only a shadow of the good things that are coming – not the realities themselves...'
Hebrews 10:1

Christians believe that Jesus offered perfect obedience in his life, perfect worship, and gave his life in a once-for-all perfect sacrifice for sin. Thus, the old rituals are redundant; now we live by grace, because of the cross and what God has done for us. This is all set out and explained in Hebrews, with the core and conclusion of the argument being in chapter ten. In the New Testament, all foods are declared clean and such religious taboos are done away with (see Mark 7:14–23 and Acts 10:9–15).

Did Moses Write the Whole Torah?

Scholars debate which parts could have been from Moses and which were collections of earlier stories and later laws added on by the early Hebrews. Also, many details could have been passed on orally before being written by later scribes, which may explain why some scholars discern the hands of various editors at work from different times; a commentary can give more details. Most agree that Moses must have had a hand in the Torah to some extent. The tradition of his involvement would not have come from nowhere, and as a former member of the Egyptian royal court, he would have been literate. It should be noted, too, that similar codes of law can be found from ancient Babylon, for example, many years before Moses would have been born. However the books were finally assembled, it is their message that counts. The stories in the Torah, though sometimes odd and primitive sounding, can be full of ethical and spiritual insights, especially if read in the light of Jesus' life and works.

Genesis

'Genesis' means 'beginnings'. The book is in two basic sections, chapters 1–11 and 12–50. The first section deals with prehistory, stories from the mists of time about the creation of the world and the early ancestors. The second section deals with the stories of the Hebrew patriarchs, Abraham, Isaac, Jacob and Joseph. They have their failings, but God works on them and with them. This book sets the stage for all that is to follow in the Bible. The world is created, humans sin and God calls certain people to make a special agreement, or covenant, with him.

'In the Beginning'

Genesis chapters 1 and 2 contain creation stories. Some interpret these symbolically, some literally. Some, for example, say that the 'days' of the creation are poetic descriptions of long periods of time – the Bible itself declares, later on, 'With the Lord a day is like a thousand years...' (2 Peter 3:8b). Some see Adam and Eve as symbolic of 'Everyman'; others view them as actual, historical human beings.

Regardless of how we interpret these stories, the point is that the Bible is saying that we are here for a purpose and not just as a result of blind chance and certain chemicals flying about. Genesis is more concerned with why we are here than how. Genesis is not intended to teach detailed and exact science, but spirituality.

The Fall

Chapter 3 is a tragedy; the first man and the first woman disobey God and follow their own whims. Spurred on by evil, or the devil, who is symbolized as a crafty serpent, they turn from life and embrace the way of death. Pain, suffering, mortality and the fear of death enter human life. Again, some take this symbolically, some literally – was there an actual Adam and Eve, or is this a parable about right and wrong choices?

The first recorded murder takes place soon after this fall from grace, as Cain kills his brother Abel out of jealousy (see Genesis 4).

The Flood

There are many versions of the Flood story that archaeologists have found in the Ancient Near East. The details are similar, but the biblical version has only one God, not many, and the reason for the flood is more moral. In the pagan versions the gods are angry because humans are noisy! In the Bible, humans have become so cruel and sinful that God seeks to wipe the slate clean and start again. Only Noah and his family are spared. God promises never to do this again.

Scientific discoveries have shown that cataclysmic, flood-type events clearly happened in the past; some think that the biblical flood was in the vicinity of the Near East, either around the Tigris and Euphrates Rivers, or around the shores of the Black Sea. The devastation of that early society would have been like the destruction of the world to them – though some do still argue for a worldwide flood.

Abraham

Genesis 11:27 – 25:11 details the career of Abraham and his wife Sarah. He receives a call from God to leave Ur and he makes his way along the fertile land surrounding the Tigris and Euphrates until he arrives in Canaan. He worships at their sacred sites (often trees) and recognizes their god El as the God who has spoken with him. He has a son, Isaac, as God promised, and another, Ishmael, through a concubine. God makes a covenant with him that through him all the nations will be blessed. Abraham's faith is severely tested when God seems to want him to sacrifice Isaac (see Genesis 22:1–14). At the last moment Isaac is spared, and Abraham learns that his God does not demand such sacrifice. This sounds like a horrid and cruel test until we realize that many gods of the surrounding tribes did demand the sacrifice of the firstborn child as a standard religious duty.

Isaac, Jacob and Esau

Isaac's story is found scattered throughout the saga of Abraham, and then in Genesis chapter 24, and 25:19 – 26:35. He marries Rebekah and has twins, Jacob and Esau. Esau is the firstborn, and rivalry always exists between the two boys. The saga of Jacob and Esau is found in Genesis chapter 25:19–34, and then in chapters 27–35. Esau sells his birthright to Jacob for a pot of stew when he is famished, and while Isaac is on his deathbed, Jacob tricks him into giving him his blessing. Jacob flees from the furious Esau and only makes peace with him much later in life. Jacob meanwhile acquires two wives, Leah and Rachel, and has two encounters with God. He dreams of a ladder with angels ascending and descending (see Genesis 28:10–22), and later he wrestles with an angel (Genesis 32:22–32). After this he is chastened and changed, and is named 'Israel', 'Prince of God'.

Joseph

The rest of Genesis is taken up by the Joseph saga. Joseph, Jacob's favourite son, is sold into slavery by his jealous brothers and taken to Egypt. His many adventures there lead him into prison and then into service at the pharaoh's court. He can interpret dreams: he warns of a famine to come, and during this, his brothers arrive in Egypt. Joseph forgives them for the past, and the whole family – the Hebrews – settles in Goshen, in northern Egypt, and prospers.

KEY VERSES

'I will make you into a great nation and I will bless you;
I will make your name great, and you will be a blessing.
I will bless those who bless you, and whoever curses you I will curse;
and all peoples on earth will be blessed through you.'

Genesis 12:2–3

JESUS IN GENESIS

There are three key passages that many see as prophesying the coming of Jesus. First, there is the hope of a Redeemer after the Fall, when the serpent, or devil, is told:

'And I will put enmity between you and the woman, and between your offspring and hers; he will crush your head, and you will strike his heel.'

Genesis 3:15

Many see Jesus as the promised seed or offspring.

The second reference is when Jacob blesses his sons:

'The sceptre will not depart from Judah, nor the ruler's staff from between his feet, until he comes to whom it belongs and the obedience of the nations is his.'

Genesis 49:10

Jesus is thought to be the coming king, or messiah.

Lastly, the story of Abraham nearly sacrificing Isaac is also seen as a type of Jesus' sacrifice. In the future God will again provide a better offering; the Father will give up the Son to die upon the cross.

QUICK READ

Genesis 1–3 – the Creation and Fall

Genesis 6–7 – the Flood

Genesis 12 – the Call of Abram

Genesis 22 – the Sacrifice of Isaac

Genesis 25:19–34 – Jacob and Esau

Genesis 28:10–22 – Jacob's Dream

Genesis 37 – Joseph's Dreams

Genesis 41–45 – Joseph's Story

Exodus

'Exodus' means 'going up' or 'going out'. The book is about a great escape, the escape of the Hebrew slaves from Egypt, led by the prophet Moses. The book of Exodus sets out the story from the beginning of slavery to the plagues, the escape, the crossing of the sea, and the giving of the Law. Various laws follow, including the Ten Commandments. Foundational themes are found here, such as the covenant, atoning sacrifice and the tabernacle.

When?

Scholars debate when the Exodus took place, and estimates range from the 16th century BC to the 13th century BC, depending on how the reigns of the pharaohs are dated. There are various clues and hints in archaeology that might fit the Exodus, such as the ancient Egyptian city of Avaris suddenly being emptied of its Semitic (Hebrew?) workers. Royal Egyptian records never spoke of defeats, and so we have very little to go on. What is striking is that the story of having been slaves is told at all; other peoples would have tried to forget this. This adds credibility to the story.

Slaves

Chapter 1 depicts the fall of the Hebrews into a condition of slavery. The close of the book of Genesis had presented a very different scenario, as they were a favoured people. Once Joseph and the pharaoh who had favoured him are dead, the Hebrews are treated as troublesome immigrants. The story surrounding the birth of Moses is horrible; an act of infant genocide is perpetrated against the Hebrews.

Moses

Exodus 2 explains how someone who was Hebrew by birth rises to favour in the Egyptian court at a time of such discrimination. The method of hiding a baby in a reed basket on a river might have been a common occurrence, for it is recorded that the Assyrian ruler, Sargon, had his life spared thus as a child.

The name 'Moses' is explained in the Old Testament text as a play on the Hebrew for 'drawn out' – i.e. 'one who was drawn out of the water'. Some scholars suggest it really has an Egyptian root, *mss*, 'one who is born' – the ending of a fuller name that would have involved one of the Egyptian deities. 'Rameses', for example, means 'Son of Ra'. Did Moses drop the pagan god's name when he turned to God?

The Call

Exodus 3 describes the call of Moses when he sees a bush that blazes with holy fire. This is a visionary experience, for the actual bush is not harmed at all. It is a passage pregnant with symbolism that speaks of the holy, mysterious otherness of God in his almighty power. Moses is called to go back to his people; he has to confront his fears after he has fled from Pharaoh.

Yahweh

In Exodus, God calls himself by a new name. He is 'Yahweh' (sometimes shortened to 'Yah'), meaning 'I am who I am' (see Exodus 3:14). The Jews treat this name as sacred and will not pronounce it. They substitute 'the Lord' instead. Before this, the general Semitic name for God, 'El', was used by the Hebrews.

The Plagues

Ten plagues confront Pharaoh and the Egyptians:

1. Rivers of blood
2. Frogs
3. Lice
4. Insects
5. Animal diseases
6. Boils
7. Hail
8. Locusts

9. Darkness

10. The death of the firstborn

It is possible that God worked through natural forces to bring these plagues; scholars speculate about what might have caused them. A drought might have spawned the curses, and similar things have been recorded at such times in the ancient history of Egypt. The water of the Nile would turn red with clay deposits; frogs would be all over searching for water; insects and infections would abound as people did not wash, and freak weather conditions that brought drought might end it suddenly with winds bringing swarms of locusts, dark clouds and storms. Others suggest that pollution killed all the fish in the Nile, and their blood made it flow red, with frogs, insects, and viral infections following. The only plague that has a deeper mystery about it is the death of the firstborn.

Passover

The Hebrews are told to clothe themselves ready for a journey, and to eat a meal of unleavened bread and lamb in their homes. Blood from the slaughtered lambs is to be smeared over their doorposts as a protection from the final plague, so that the Hebrew children will be spared (see Exodus 12). The Jews still celebrate the Passover meal annually, recalling their time as slaves and the great liberation that came.

Freedom

Moses and the Hebrews escape, but Pharaoh goes back on his word and gives chase. The slaves escape through the Sea of Reeds (often translated 'Red Sea,' but the Hebrew text has 'Yam Suph', the 'Sea of Reeds'). This stretch of water would have been a large, marshy lake north of the Red Sea. Exodus 14:21–22 describes this occurrence, which would not have been as instant and as dramatic as Hollywood films suggest! A strong wind blew all night, moving the waters. Some suggest that this was a tsunami, a huge tidal wave set off by a volcanic eruption on the Greek island of Santorini. Water could have been drawn back for a couple of hours, and then the wave would have come crashing in. Whatever the forces involved, the miracle was certainly in the timing. The Hebrews got through; the Egyptians did not. The Song of Miriam in Exodus 15 is thought to be a very early poem about this pivotal event.

The Law and the Covenant

Moses assembles the Hebrew tribes at Mount Sinai (or Horeb in other traditions in the Bible). After a period of separation from them on the mountain, when he goes to be alone with God, he descends with the Ten Commandments written on tablets of stone. In Exodus 21–23 there are early collections of additional laws for the community. The rest of the book describes the tabernacle, its layout and how to offer worship there. The tabernacle was a tent with a holy place within, which only the high priest (at first, Moses' brother Aaron) could enter. The wandering Hebrews carried this with them wherever they went.

The tabernacle contained the ark of the covenant. The ark was a wooden box that was overlaid with gold and had a lid bearing two kneeling angels whose wing tips touched. This box contained the tablets of the Law. The presence of God was over this object, as a powerful focus of his majesty on earth. It was treated with great fear and reverence, and was a reminder of the covenant, the binding promise that if the Hebrews served the Lord alone, he would be their God. One sign of keeping the covenant was the circumcision of male children eight days after birth.

The Golden Calf

Exodus 32 describes the rejection of belief, or apostasy, of the people, who are tired of waiting for Moses as he communes with God on the mountain. They persuade Aaron to make them an image to worship, the golden calf. Bull-type images were common in the Ancient Near East to represent deity, suggesting virility and power. The Ten Commandments had expressly forbidden making such an image, partly because the true God was invisible Spirit, and partly because the ancients believed that having an image of a god gave them a measure of control over it. When Moses returns, he breaks the tablets in protest and has the calf destroyed. The covenant with God has then to be renewed after a period of repentance.

Mine Eyes Have Seen the Glory!

A moving and curious passage occurs in Exodus 33:18–23. Moses asks to see the glory of God, a manifestation of his invisible presence. He is told to hide in the cleft of a rock until the glory has passed by, and then he can catch a fleeting glimpse. God says, 'Then I will remove my hand and you will see my back; but my face must not be seen.' This is poetic language; the 'face' of God is not a literal face, but the full-blown revelation of his glory, which would have made Moses fall down dead. The 'back' is a fading vision, a slight opening of the veil between material and spiritual worlds.

KEY VERSE

'God said to Moses, "I AM who I AM. This is what you are to say to the Israelites: 'I AM has sent me to you.'"'

Exodus 3:14

JESUS IN EXODUS

A so-called 'type' of Christ is found in the sacrificed lambs whose blood daubed the doorposts and whose flesh was eaten within. Jesus is known to Christians as 'the Lamb of God' who takes away the sins of the world. Under his blood those who believe in him find spiritual protection and forgiveness, and they are to feed on him in their hearts by faith through his Word and sacraments, such as the holy communion.

A type of baptism is found in the passing through the water at the Sea of Reeds, as Paul states in 1 Corinthians 10:1–2.

QUICK READ

Exodus 3 – the Call of Moses

Exodus 7–11 – the Ten Plagues

Exodus 12 – the Passover Meal

Exodus 14 – the Crossing of the Sea of Reeds

Exodus 20 – the Ten Commandments

Leviticus

Leviticus is a book about rituals, describing types of sacrifice and priestly robes, as well as a deeper and wider look at what holiness requires – a lifestyle of compassion.

Leviticus contains no stories about Moses and the Hebrews leaving Egypt or wandering around the desert. It is all prescriptions about how to worship and how to be holy. 'Holiness' in Hebrew thought can mean 'wholeness, health, purity and righteousness'. Leviticus can seem hopelessly antiquated and esoteric to modern eyes, but there are rich symbols and undercurrents in there.

Be Holy…

Anything imperfect cannot be offered to God. An animal with a blemish or a disease must not be brought to the tabernacle. Disabled people, foreigners and eunuchs cannot serve at its altar. Women during their menstrual period are also barred.

This sounds harsh, but the ritual laws taught perfection and a view of holiness. It is important to recall that eunuchs and the disabled, as well as foreigners, were welcomed by God in themselves even if not in the tabernacle. Leviticus 19:33–34 reminds people to be kind to the strangers in their land, for the Hebrews were once strangers in Egypt. Isaiah 56:3–7 explains that eunuchs and strangers who follow the Torah in their hearts are loved by God.

At the end of the book, it is seen that holiness demands a certain way of life, too. The Holiness Code, which can be found in chapter 19, covers many ethical precepts such as not stealing and not hating one's neighbour. It also warns against dishonest business practices. Other topics concern not seeking the help of mediums or necromancers, as this can open the way to dangerous spiritual forces.

Jubilee

Later in the book the land itself is to be the subject of holiness. Leviticus 25 speaks of the sabbatical year and the Jubilee. The former is a commandment to let land lie fallow every seven years, and the Jubilee is every 50 years. On the Jubilee year, lands are to be returned to their rightful owners, slaves are to be freed, and debts are to be cancelled. These are radical recipes for environmental and social justice unparalled in the ancient world.

Food

Leviticus 11 presents lists of clean and unclean food (kosher and unkosher). This seems strange to modern sentiments, though many Jews still keep the food laws as they see them as a way of maintaining their cultural identity. Scholars point out that these laws were probably for health reasons in the beginning. For example, animals that do not chew the cud are generally scavengers, eating all sorts of rubbish; pork is an easily infected meat; and shellfish can carry bacterial infection. On a spiritual level, these rules can remind us that to be holy is to be healthy. These food laws were set aside by the early church, which believed that all things created by God were clean (see Mark 7:14–23 and Acts 10:9–16).

Sacrifice

Reading through Leviticus 1–5, we see that the main types of offering are the burnt offering, the grain offering, the peace offering, the sin offering and the guilt offering.

1. Burnt – bulls, lambs, doves and pigeons could be offered totally, i.e. burnt up on the altar. These were offered morning and evening in the tabernacle.

2. Grain – grain, flour, oil, unleavened bread and salt could be offered as simple acts of worship.

3. Peace – any animal could be offered as a sign of fellowship, accompanied by a communal feast. Much of the meat was eaten by the worshippers.

4. Sin – these were offered to atone for unintentional sins, usually using bulls, goats or lambs.

5. Guilt – a ram or lamb was offered to make peace after knowingly committing a sin. Compensation was also to be paid to the person wronged.

This elaborate system taught the people holiness and covered various aspects of their lives. The sacrifices were joyful procedures (not for the animals!) that allowed them to worship God and also taught the costliness of forgiveness and sin – lives were taken and blood was shed. In the New Testament, Jesus is seen to fulfil many of the offerings in his own person. He offered his life up totally, dying on a cross; he lived a life of worship to the Father; he made peace between God and humanity by his blood; and he offered his life as an atonement for sin, both intentional and unintentional.

Day of Atonement

A sacrifice was offered for the whole community once a year. One goat was sacrificed and another was sent into exile into the desert after the high priest had laid his hands upon it and confessed the sins of the people over it. This ritual does not continue among modern Jews, but the Day of Atonement, or Yom Kippur, is a day of repentance and reflection, a day of spiritual spring cleaning. Again, in the New Testament, Jesus is seen as fulfilling this ritual, offering himself once for all.

KEY VERSE

'Be holy because I, the Lord your God, am holy.'

Leviticus 19:2

JESUS IN LEVITICUS

Jesus is the fulfilment of all the sacrifices for sin and to make peace. The Epistle to the Hebrews declares: 'And by that will, we have been made holy through the sacrifice of the body of Jesus Christ once for all' Hebrews 10:10.

QUICK READ

Leviticus 1–5 – Sacrifices for Sin and for Worship

Leviticus 11 – the Food Laws

Leviticus 16 – the Day of Atonement

Leviticus 19 – the Holiness Code

Leviticus 25:8–end – the Jubilee

Numbers

Numbers is about more than lists of tribes and descendants; it is also about the journeys of the Israelites in the Sinai Desert.

In the Desert

The Hebrew name for the book of Numbers, 'BeMidbar', means 'in the desert', which is perhaps a more accurate description of what the book is about when you get past the lists of Numbers 1–3 and the ritual details in Numbers 4–9. Some interesting items in these chapters concern the role of the Levites, a tribe set apart for service in the tabernacle, and the priestly or Aaronic blessing, often used in Christian worship (see Numbers 6:22–26). Also, there is the Nazirite vow whereby a person is dedicated to the Lord, never touching alcohol and never cutting their hair (see Numbers 6:1–21). 'Nazir' meant 'to vow', and Samson was a famous Nazirite.

Wandering

The Israelites leave Mount Sinai and begin their journey to the Promised Land of Canaan. A series of disputes and rebellions thwarts this journey – so much so that they are condemned to wander for a generation (40 years in Hebrew thought). Numbers 16 and 17 concern a major rebellion led by Korah, Dathan and Abiram against Moses and Aaron. Aaron's walking staff buds with life, bearing almond blossom, as a sign that the blessing and authority is with him and his brother, Moses.

Hebrews/Israelites

The term 'Israel' or 'Israelite' is now common; the earlier term of 'Hebrew' has been dropped. This is based on the ancestor Jacob, who was renamed 'Israel' after his encounter with God. The people were known as Israelites in records from this period.

Provision

The Israelites complain that they are short of food and water, and some of them would prefer to go back to slavery in Egypt rather than suffer in the desert. Moses prays and various answers are given – these could be regarded as supernatural or as God working through the forces of nature. Manna (literally, Hebrew for 'What is that?') appears on the ground as a white, flaky, sweet substance (could this have been insect secretions that are still found and eaten by Bedouin? The insects suck out the sap from trees and deposit the residue like glistening pearls of crystal on the ground.) (See Numbers 11:4–9.) Quails fly low to rest in the Israelite camp (Numbers 11:10–34) and provide plentiful meat. Water flows from a rock (see Numbers 20:1–13) which Moses strikes with his rod (a miracle, or the dislodging of highly porous limestone which released a stream of water?). As with the escape at the Sea of Reeds, the focus for believers may be more on the timing.

Balaam's Ass

Numbers 22–24 recounts the story of Balaam, a seer. Such people were said to be skilled in communication with the spirit world, skilled at discerning the will of the gods, and they could utter curses and blessings. The king of Moab, Balak, was trying to destroy the Israelites and so he sought Balaam's services. Balaam set out on his donkey and was stopped by an angel. He even thought he heard his ass speak! He soon realized that he could not curse Israel because God was blessing them. (Balaam and others of his time would have recognized a High God over all the gods.) Instead, he blessed Israel – four times!

Nearing Canaan

Towards the end of the book, the tribes are approaching the River Jordan. Two tribes, Reuben and Gad, wish to stay in the Transjordan area. They are allowed to stay, though they will miss out on the blessings of the Promised Land. They agree to support the other tribes with military help if needed. The Levites are not given any territory, as such, but are offered several cities of refuge to settle in. The idea was that someone suspected of a crime could flee there until their trial was heard, to stop people taking matters into their own hands.

Insights from Archaeology

Many scholars despair of the fact that no traces of the Israelite wandering in the wilderness can be found. Admittedly, they were nomadic and living in simple settlements for much of this time, but it is frustrating that nothing has been found. However, discoveries at a mountain, Jebel Ideid, in the desert are fascinating. This was an ancient gathering place with many standing stones and altars from pre-Israelite days. There is early graffiti showing hunters, but also some intriguing markings that seem to show a rod and a serpent, a shape divided into ten panels (Ten Commandments?), and many people with hands raised in prayer. These are hard to date, but could these be Israelite? Was this site the true location of Mount Sinai, or some other gathering place of worship such as at Kadesh, where the Hebrews settled for a time while wandering in the desert?

KEY VERSES

'The Lord bless you and keep you;
the Lord make his face shine upon you and be gracious to you;
the Lord turn his face towards you and give you peace.'

Numbers 6:24–26

JESUS IN NUMBERS

The apostle Paul links Jesus with Moses' desert rock that provided life-giving water in 1 Corinthians 10:3–4, saying, 'and that rock was Christ'. Balaam's oracle of blessing upon Israel mentions a leader who is to come:

'I see him, but not now;
I behold him, but not near.
A star will come out of Jacob;
a sceptre will rise out of Israel…'

Numbers 24:17

Some see this as the messiah, with the star imagery suggesting the star of Bethlehem.

QUICK READ

Numbers 6:1–21 – the Nazirite Vow

Numbers 16–17 – Rebellion and Aaron's Rod
Numbers 20:1–13 – Water from the Rock
Numbers 22–24 – Balaam

Deuteronomy

Deuteronomy (meaning 'repetition of the Law') is Moses' farewell to the people, reminding them of the Torah and renewing their commitment to it.

Farewell

The feel of this book is more mature, reflective and sensitive to God's love and mercy than other sections of the Torah. This could, indeed, come from the mature thoughts of Moses before his death. Some scholars wonder if the final form of this book was written much later, when the young King Josiah discovered a book of the Law and led a movement of repentance and renewal (see 2 Kings 22:1–20). Whatever the truth of this, much of the material is likely to have come from Moses and this work is spilling over with inspiration and insight.

Moses recaps the history of the people and God's care for them, reminding them of the pains of disobedience. Moses himself is forbidden to cross the River Jordan (Deuteronomy 3:21–29). Joshua is to be his successor.

The Ten Commandments

A second version of the Ten Commandments is found in Deuteronomy 5:6–21, with the only difference being the reason given for keeping the sabbath day. In Deuteronomy it is because the Israelites were brought out of slavery in Egypt; in Exodus it is because God created the world in six days and rested on the seventh.

One Holy Place

Deuteronomy 12 orders that there should be one place for the tabernacle and that all other pagan holy places should be destroyed. This is different from other books of the Torah, and the early Israelites wandered around with the tabernacle tent for some time, not resting it in one place only. This could be Moses looking ahead to a time when the people were settled in the land, or it could reflect conditions of Josiah's time (see earlier).

The same debate is held over instructions to appoint a king (see Deuteronomy 17:14–20). Essentially, either Moses foresaw that this would be needed, or these are later laws.

The Occult and Prophets

Deuteronomy condemns the use of occult powers as dangerous and idolatrous. Deuteronomy 18:9–13 lists a number of these items, such as contacting spirits of the dead (mediums), using witchcraft, practising spells, and studying omens and divination (foretelling the future). These are all said to be an abomination to the Lord. They seek out forces and powers that do not come from God. Such occult practices usually seek to control and to manipulate events. Deuteronomy 18:14–15 promises that God will raise up prophets to guide Israel instead. Later, in Deuteronomy 29:29, we read: 'The secret things belong to the Lord our God, but the things revealed belong to us and to our children for ever, that we may follow all the words of this law.'

Blessings and Curses

Deuteronomy 28 lists a number of blessings and curses that will come upon the people for following or disobeying the Torah. Christians claim these blessings as members of the new covenant and part of the Body of Christ, saying that the blessings are their inheritance, too. Deuteronomy follows this theme throughout the book – that the righteous person will find blessing in this life.

Death of Moses

Chapter 32 presents the lyrical Song of Moses, which recounts the history of Israel's salvation in poetic form. This could be a very ancient part of the text of this book. After blessing each of the tribes, Moses ascends a hill, looks across to the land of Canaan, and then dies in Moab. No one knows where he is buried, which gives rise to later speculations that God had simply taken him, like Enoch and Elijah. Moses is honoured as the greatest prophet the Israelites ever had.

KEY VERSE

'Hear, O Israel: The Lord our God, the Lord is one. Love the Lord your God with all your heart and with all your soul and with all your strength.'

Deuteronomy 6:4–5

JESUS IN DEUTERONOMY

Jesus is the prophet par excellence who will be raised up after Moses (see Deuteronomy 18:15). God spoke in many ways, but his final word is through the Son (see Hebrews 1:1–2).

QUICK READ

Deuteronomy 5:6–21 – the Ten Commandments

Deuteronomy 18:9–13 – the Dangers of the Occult

Deuteronomy 28:1–14 – Blessings

Deuteronomy 30:15–20 – the Appeal to Choose Life

The History Books

The Hebrew Bible contains 12 history books. These are accounts of particular individuals (such as Ruth) or histories of kings and battles. There are reforms, revolutions, high adventure, murders and prophetic oracles. Much of this material would have been oral tradition, passed on by word of mouth as the tales of the people. It is thought that the book of Ruth, though based on old stories, might have been written down relatively late, to make a point to the people of that day. There are two different versions of the history of the people and their kings, one found in the books of Kings and the other in the books of Chronicles.

Various sources are mentioned in these, such as the book of the Chronicles of the Kings of Israel, and the book of the Chronicles of the Kings of Judah. These were probably king lists as found in other ancient societies. There is also the book of Jashar (see 2 Samuel 1:18), which probably contained poems and songs. These books have been lost. The theology of the writer of Deuteronomy is present, for when kings obey the Lord, they are blessed, and when they rebel, disaster strikes the land.

Joshua

The book of Joshua tells the story of how the Israelites entered the Promised Land, of the initial battles and struggles, the allotment of land to the tribes, and the renewal of the covenant.

Encouragement

Joshua 1 is a promise and an encouragement from God to Joshua to go forward in faith and courage. God will be with the people and none may stand against them, as long as Joshua does not depart from the Torah. 'Have I not commanded you?' says God to Joshua. 'Be strong and courageous. Do not be terrified, do not be discouraged, for the Lord your God will be with you wherever you go' (Joshua 1:9).

Rahab

Joshua 2 tells the story of Rahab the prostitute. Rahab probably kept an inn and offered her sexual services. She helps Israelite spies in Jericho. She hides them and allows them to escape from her window, which is set in the city wall. She pledges herself to support Israel and the spies warn her to keep her family in the house when they attack, and to tie a scarlet cord from her window. She and her family are spared (see Joshua 6:22–25). That a prostitute was allotted a place with the people of God shows the inclusiveness and mercy of the Lord.

Crossing the Jordan

Joshua 3–4 has the priests leading the procession across the Jordan. They are told to step out in faith and the waters of the river will dry up. Indeed, the Bible records, 'Yet as soon as the priests who carried the ark reached the Jordan and their feet touched the water's edge, the water from upstream stopped flowing. It piled up in a heap a great distance away…' (Joshua 3:15b–16a). There it stays until all the tribes have crossed.

This might have been caused by a landslide at the source of the river. An Arab historian recorded a similar phenomenon in AD 1266. The miracle would then be, again, in the timing.

Joshua then circumcises any men who had not been circumcised as babies. They had not been circumcised in the desert, and all the men of military age who had come out of Egypt had died before reaching Canaan. The Lord declares that he has rolled the reproach of Egypt off them.

The Walls of Jericho

After an angelic vision (see Joshua 5:13–15), Joshua prepares to attack the fortified city of Jericho. Such walled cities controlled the land, placing power in the hands of the local kings. Some scholars suggest that these cities were exploiting the local farmers, many of whom were related to the Israelites, anyway. The Israelites circle the walls once each day, praising God. On the seventh day they march round the city seven times, and the walls fall. The whole place is destroyed and burned – buildings, possessions, people and cattle. Only Rahab and her family are spared.

This story raises a couple of issues:

Firstly, was it a miracle?

Archaeologists have found evidence of an early city on the site that was destroyed by an earthquake, and then invaders burned the place, leaving a layer of ash. There are debates about how these ruins should be dated, but this certainly fits the biblical account. Was the event supernatural or God working through natural forces? The miracle, once again, would have been in the timing – just as the Israelites marched for the seventh time, the earthquake struck.

Secondly, did God really want all the people and cattle killed?

Joshua placed the city 'under the ban', or *haram* in Hebrew. This was a custom sometimes used when a city had opposed an attacker. It was a judgment. Today we would call this an act of genocide and condemn it as a war crime.

Perhaps we need to remember that this all took place a long, long time before Jesus, when so little was understood about God. This is a very early story in the Old Testament, from a time when people were more primitive. Many Jews struggle with the issues surrounding this story, too. Sometimes people read a spiritual or allegorical message into it, even though its literal meaning is quite horrible. The message is that we must ruthlessly put to death all that is sinful within us.

The Sin of Achan

Joshua 7 tells of the sin of Achan. The Israelites become overconfident and attack the city of Ai. They are routed and Joshua assembles the tribes. Achan and his family are found to have disobeyed the order to destroy everything in Jericho. They have taken and hidden some treasures. These are destroyed and Achan's family are stoned to death. In Joshua 8 Ai is attacked again and this time defeated.

This also seems to be a harsh and horrible story. Again, however, we are dealing with primitive times before the mercy and forgiveness taught by the later prophets, or declared in the new covenant. Using this story allegorically, we can see how we need to root out sin, demolishing all deceptions, and deal with it. If not, it will spoil and pollute our walk with God.

Shechem

After many chapters detailing more battles and how land is to be given out to the tribes, Joshua 24 has a renewal ceremony at Shechem. Here, the tribes assemble and Joshua recounts the history of God's saving acts. The tribes are asked whom they serve and they swear to serve the Lord. Joshua sets up a stone at Shechem as a testament to this oath (which might still exist in the ruins of a temple and fortification in the modern city of Nablus).

The need for regular renewals may not have been just to prevent idolatory, but also to unite the tribes who could, potentially, seek to act alone.

KEY VERSE

'But if serving the Lord seems undesirable to you, then choose for yourselves this day whom you will serve… But as for me and my household, we will serve the Lord.'

Joshua 24:15

JESUS IN JOSHUA

Early Christian writers saw in Rahab's scarlet cord a reference to the red blood of Christ, which saves us and covers us with mercy.

A second possible type of Christ is the vision of the captain of the Lord's army (Joshua 5:13–15). Some see this as the pre-incarnate Christ, others as an angelic presence.

A third, and more general idea of Christ is in the imagery of Joshua (whose name is a variant of 'Jesus', meaning 'God saves') leading the people through the Jordan into the Promised Land. Christians believe Jesus leads us through death to the glory of heaven.

QUICK READ

Joshua 1 – Blessing, Challenge and Encouragement for the Future
Joshua 2 – the Story of Rahab
Joshua 3 – the Crossing of the Jordan
Joshua 6 – the Fall of Jericho
Joshua 7 – the Sin of Achan
Joshua 24 – the Renewal of the Covenant at Shechem

Judges and Ruth

Judges deals with the years after the death of Joshua. The tribes were often disunited and turned to the worship of Canaanite gods such as Ba'al, a fertility deity. The judges were charismatic leaders, raised up directly by God to lead the tribes into battle or to settle everyday disputes.

Ruth is a short story set in the time of the judges, and it deals with a destitute mother and daughter-in-law and the relative who comes to their aid. It is also a story of unexpected love.

THE TWELVE JUDGES

The twelve recorded judges are Othniel, Ehud, Shamgar, Deborah, Gideon, Tola, Jair, Jephthah, Ibzan, Elon, Abdon and Samson. Very little is known about some of them – such as Tola, even though he was a judge for 23 years! Deborah was the only woman.

Trouble

The Canaanites had not been completely defeated by Joshua, and they regrouped under the leadership of Jabin, king of Hazor. There were also troublesome neighbours such as Moab, or the Midianites from the desert. Then there were the newly settled Philistines along the coastal plain. Hence, there were many battles and the need for leaders.

Judges is a depressing and violent book at times. Ehud killed an obese king when he was on the toilet, and he was so fat that Ehud could not retrieve his sword from his belly! Shamgar killed 600 Philistines with an ox-goad. The author comments that the people often did what was right in their own sight. There was lawlessness, moral relativism and idolatory. This violent age was primitive, and a long time before Jesus or later Old Testament ideas.

Deborah

Judges 4:1 – 5:31 tells the story of the only female judge. She goes into battle with the Israelite military commander, Barak, against Jabin's forces, which are led by the commander Sisera. Sisera flees and hides in the tent of another man's wife, Jael. Little does he know that this family sides with Israel, and Jael kills him while he is sleeping by driving a tent-peg through his head! The Song of Deborah is a very ancient composition, and some of these old stories were probably passed down through folk songs.

Gideon

Judges 6:1 – 8:35 tells the story of Gideon, a reluctant leader. He leads a force of 300 men into battle against the Midianites. He reduces his potential army from 32,000 by God's guidance, an act which provides a parable on trust in spiritual help and not human might. A clever trick defeats the Midianites with the aid of clay pots and torches at night. The people seek to make Gideon their king – they are lusting after the style of government of their pagan neighbours to unify them. He refuses, saying that only the Lord must rule over them. He takes gold earrings and makes some sort of cult object. He erects this in his home town (perhaps to commemorate his victory), but the people worship it as an idol.

Jephthah

Judges 11:1 – 12:7 tells the story of Jephthah. He rescues his people from the Philistines and the Midianites, but he makes a very foolish vow before the battle: he will sacrifice the first living thing that he sees on his return home. It happens to be his daughter, and, unbelievably, he goes through with this! This was not a vow acceptable to God, but it shows us how primitive these times were, and how darkened people's understanding of God was. Many neighbouring cultures practised child sacrifice.

Samson

Judges 13:1 – 16:31 tells the story of Samson. He is a Nazirite, one who is dedicated to the Lord from birth and is never to drink alcohol or cut his hair. The Spirit of the Lord – the presence and power of God – is said to come upon him and make him a mighty man. He is a Hebrew version of the Greek Heracles, or our modern-day superheroes. He is pitted against the Philistines, but he falls for a Philistine woman, Delilah, who seduces him and seeks to betray him. He refuses to reveal the secret of his power until, in a moment of weakness, he tells her about his vow never to cut his hair. She cuts it, his power leaves him, and he is captured, blinded and humiliated. Gradually the hair grows back and his strength returns. He enacts his revenge by pushing apart the pillars of a pagan temple and killing many people. His story is also primitive and disturbing, a far cry from the ethical prophets that come later, or the beauty of the New Testament. Nonetheless, he shows human frailty in his lusts and how God's blessing often works with and through the unworthy and the wayward.

KEY VERSE

'In those days Israel had no king; everyone did as he saw fit.'

Judges 17:6

JESUS IN JUDGES

The coming of the Spirit upon ordinary men and women to make them great warriors or wise leaders is seen as prefiguring the anointing of Jesus with the Spirit as messiah. His task was far greater – a task that no mere mortal could ever achieve. He was to bring reconciliation between God and humanity.

Also, the conclusion of the Song of Deborah declares, 'But may they who love you be like the sun when it rises in its strength.' Jesus was known as the 'sun of righteousness' by early Christian writers, recalling the promise of salvation in Malachi 4:2. Jesus is said to be the light of the world that the darkness cannot overcome (see John 1:5).

QUICK READ

Judges 2:1–5 – the Angel of the Lord Rebukes Israel
Judges 4–5 – the Story of Deborah
Judges 6–8 – the Story of Gideon
Judges 13–16 – the Story of Samson

RUTH

Destitution

Elimelech and his wife, Naomi, take refuge in neighbouring Moab when a famine strikes. Elimelech dies, as do his two sons. They leave behind two widows, Moabite women, Ruth and Orpah. Naomi seeks to return to Canaan when she hears that the famine is over. She frees the girls of any obligation to attend to her. Ruth pleads to go back with her, and swears that Naomi's God will now be her God.

Boaz

Ruth and Naomi return to Naomi's ancestral home in Bethlehem, and Ruth is sent to glean in the fields belonging to a kinsman, Boaz. (The poor were allowed to pick up any grain that had been left on the ground by the harvesters.) Ruth comes to Boaz's attention, and when he sleeps on the threshing floor late in the harvesting time, Ruth lies at his feet. By doing this she shows her submission and loyalty, as well as requesting his aid. Boaz agrees to 'redeem' her, following an ancient custom whereby a next of kin could marry a widow and raise offspring to carry on the family line.

Truths to tell...

The word 'redemption' occurs in the short book of Ruth 23 times! This is a social redemption, rather than a spiritual one. Ruth and her mother-in-law are to be cared and provided for. Boaz is a 'kinsman-redeemer', one who comes to their aid.

That a foreign woman could be embraced by God's covenant was important – this combated racism and any haughty ideas that the Israelites might have had. Ruth was also an ancestor of King David, the great king of the Jewish people. Foreign blood flowed in David's veins.

Interestingly, God is rarely mentioned in the book, apart from Ruth's pledge of service at the start.

KEY VERSE

'Where you go I will go, and where you stay I will stay. Your people will be my people and your God my God.'

Ruth 1:16b

JESUS IN RUTH

Boaz is a type of Christ as the redeemer of the human race. Christian theology says we are destitute in our sinfulness and in need of grace and mercy. Through the blood of the cross, Jesus becomes our 'kinsman-redeemer'.

QUICK READ

Ruth 1:8–18 – Ruth's Pledge of Loyalty
Ruth 2:5–13 – Ruth is Noticed by Boaz
Ruth 3:7–14 – Ruth Lies at Boaz's Feet
Ruth 4:6–10 – Ruth is Redeemed
Ruth 4:18–22 – the Genealogy of David

1 and 2 Samuel

The two books of Samuel tell the story of the rise of Israel's monarchy, especially the exploits of King David. During this time, Jerusalem became the capital city and the ark of God was brought there. A nation was forged from the federation of tribes.

The Birth and Call of Samuel

Chapters 1 and 2 detail the prayers made by Hannah, a barren woman. She gives birth to a son and dedicates him to the service of the Lord by giving him over to the care of the priests at the tabernacle in Shiloh. Eli is the priest, and his sons were wayward and corrupt. The priests would raise orphans or dedicated children and the boys would serve as priests later. Hannah's song is similar to Mary's song, the Magnificat, particularly the expression about lifting the lowly (see 1 Samuel 2:8). The name 'Samuel' means 'offspring of El', El being an ancient name for God.

As a young boy, Samuel is awakened by a voice which he thinks is Eli's. It is actually the Lord's – a rare example of verbal communication with God. Sometimes people hear such a divine voice, but God's communication is usually non-verbal, in the heart and spirit, or through the words of the Bible.

The Ark is Captured

First Samuel 4–6 tell the story of the capture of the ark and its return. The enemy here are the Philistines, part of an immigrant group from the Mediterranean known to scholars and ancient texts as 'the Sea Peoples'. They occupied the coastal plain and towns. The Israelites held the hill country, which was not as prosperous an area, and which was regarded as a poor backwater by the surrounding nations.

First Samuel 5 describes how disaster and plague come upon the Philistines because they have the ark, whose holiness can curse as well as bless. The god Dagon's statue falls down and breaks before the ark. Their priests and soothsayers eventually order them to send it back, harnessed to oxen but guided by no human hand. The oxen stop at Beth-Shemesh, where the ark is placed on a rock and the oxen are slaughtered and offered in sacrifice. In 1 Samuel 7, Samuel assembles the tribes at Mizpah and fasts and repents before the Lord. The Philistines come to attack, but violent thunder terrifies them and they retreat.

Samuel is acting as a judge by this time, travelling around. He was to be one of the last judges.

The King

The elders of Israel come to the aged Samuel at Ramah and beg him to give them a king. God speaks to Samuel and tells him to give the people their heart's desire. Samuel tells the elders what this will mean in a provocative passage in 1 Samuel 8:10–18. A monarch will have privileges and wealth that will set him apart. It is God's plan B for Israel, for his plan A had himself as the king and the people all equal to one another under him.

Saul

First Samuel chapters 9–10 tell the story about the choice of Saul as king. 'Saul' was probably not his original name as it meant 'asked for', and he was asked for by the people. This could have been a coronation name. His real name might have been 'Labaya' ('Great Lion of Yah') – more on this later. Saul goes to Samuel for his services as a 'seer' – a holy man who could hear from God – because Saul has lost his donkeys. Samuel, however, has a revelation, a word of knowledge from God, that Saul is to be the chosen king. Samuel eats with him and privately anoints him with oil. The assembled tribes later choose Saul by casting lots. Saul springs into action straight away by leading the tribes against the Ammonite king, Nahash (1 Samuel 11).

Saul's Apostasy

Saul begins to act independently of Samuel's advice and the law of Moses. He is waiting at Gilgal for Samuel to come to offer sacrifices. Samuel is late and some of the soldiers begin to desert, so Saul panics and offers the sacrifices himself. Samuel condemns him for this and prophesies that his monarchy will come to an end (1 Samuel 13:11–14, and reaffirmed in 1 Samuel 15:10–31).

His decline is sealed by a further act of disobedience. In 1 Samuel 28 Saul is scared by the vast forces being assembled by the Philistines and he finds no guidance from God. He seeks out a necromancer, one who consults the spirits of the dead (a medium, in modern parlance). He finds such a woman at Endor, and she calls forth the spirit of Samuel, who then curses Saul for daring to do such a forbidden thing. The Law forbids necromancy as a dangerous pursuit that can tamper with spiritual forces best left undisturbed. (Note: the text suggests that she really has called up Samuel's ghost – it isn't a trick or an imposter spirit.)

David

In 1 Samuel 16 the Lord leads Samuel to the house of Jesse in Bethlehem. He meets all of Jesse's sons, but he knows that none of them is to be the next king. There is one other, the youngest, David, who returns from the fields after watching the sheep. God tells Samuel not to look at the outward appearance, for God knows the heart. Samuel takes David and anoints him privately with holy oil. 'David', again, might not have been his original name, but a later coronation title meaning 'Beloved of Yah'. His real name might have been 'Elhanan' ('El shows favour'), according to the interpretations of certain archaeologists. David enters Saul's service, where he plays soothing music on his harp to calm the depressed and afflicted king.

Goliath

First Samuel 17 tells the story of Goliath's challenge to the Israelite army. In those days, challenges to a fight between individual warriors as champions for their nations was not unusual, as is seen in the Greek stories of Homer. Goliath is described as being about 3 metres tall, which is not impossible and not at all like somebody out of *Jack and the Beanstalk*. David accepts the challenge and slays the mighty warrior with a stone from his shepherd's sling. This shows that the grace and calling of God are more powerful than oceans of human skill; with the power of the Spirit, the simple and the humble can go where no one else can tread.

David, Jonathan and the Outlaws

First Samuel chapters 18–20 relate how a close friendship develops between David and Saul's son Jonathan. David marries

Saul's daughter, Michal, thus becoming Saul's son-in-law. Saul, more depressed than ever, becomes jealous of David's successful attacks on the Philistines. David has to flee for his life and hide out in the hills with a band of outlaws and mercenaries. He has a chance to kill Saul when hiding in a cave, but spares him (see 1 Samuel 24:1–13). David and 600 men eventually take refuge with King Achish of Gath, a Philistine ruler. David is prepared to fight against Saul with him, but the Philistines send his band away, fearing that he might change sides. The Philistines attack Saul on Mount Gilboa, and archers kill the leaders of Israel, including Saul and Jonathan. The Philistines behead them and hang the torsos on the walls of the city of Beth-Shan.

A Light from Archaeology?

The Armana letters, a series of clay tablets sent from Canaanite rulers to the Egyptian pharaoh, are usually thought to refer to the conquest period when the Israelite tribes were raiding and attacking Canaan. Some scholars now date these much later, placing them in the reigns of Saul and David where, in fact, the details fit much better. They mention 'Labaya' as the king of the 'Habiru' ('wanderers', and obviously similar to 'Hebrew'), and 'Elhanan' as their second king. There are possible parallels with some of the stories, as well as a number of names that might be similar to biblical characters. A small clay inscription has been found at Beth-Shan (where Saul's body was hung) bearing the name 'Labaya'. Curiously, too, in 2 Samuel 21:19, Elhanan is named as the slayer of Goliath! If this dating is correct, these documents provide an independent verification for much of the material in 1 and 2 Samuel.

David the King

In the early chapters of 2 Samuel, David is recognized as the king of the tribe of Judah after Saul's death. The other tribes, calling themselves, collectively, 'Israel', choose another of Saul's sons, Ish-Bosheth. David is attached to the Philistine ruler, Achish, and his tribe is thus seen as being out of the federation of tribes. He makes Hebron his capital and rules from there for seven and a half years. The saga continues, with David getting wives, siring children and fighting many battles. It is rousing but bloodthirsty stuff, and still far from Jesus both in time and theology. For some time David's men and Israel work in parallel, until the forces meet at the Pool of Gibeon. Their champions fight and kill each other, and a free-for-all follows. The Israelite general, Abner, kills the brother of Joab, David's commander. This leads to a bloody feud, and Joab slyly kills Abner as David is making overtures for peace. Ish-Bosheth is murdered in his bed and the head is brought to David. In disgust, David has the killers executed.

Jerusalem

Jerusalem is controlled by the Jebusites, and is reputed to be invulnerable. David sends a party of men into the city through the underground drinking water channels, surprising the people in their beds. The Jebusites' mockery (2 Samuel 5:6) ultimately rings hollow, and later believers draw a spiritual lesson from this, which is that when God speaks against a stronghold of the enemy, it can and will fall if people are faithful. David then makes Jerusalem his capital, has a palace built for himself and erects the tabernacle tent for the ark there. His desire to build a permanent temple for the Lord is rejected by the prophet Nathan (2 Samuel 7); rather, one of David's sons will build a temple and his line will reign for ever. David dances before the ark when it is brought into Jerusalem, wearing only a linen tunic. His wife, Michal, scorns him for this display, but in the joy of the Lord there is no disgrace (see 2 Samuel 6:14–23).

Bathsheba

Second Samuel chapters 11–12 tell the story of David's adultery with Bathsheba, the wife of Uriah the Hittite. He watches her bathing, sends for her, and she becomes pregnant with David's child. David tries to conceal his adultery by bringing Uriah home from the battle, getting him drunk and trying to send him home to Bathsheba. However, Uriah stays with the guards, not wishing to go to his wife when his men are still fighting. David then tells Joab to send Uriah into the thick of the fighting, ensuring that he will be killed. He then marries Bathsheba and she has a son.

The prophet Nathan comes to the king and tells him the parable of the shepherd and his lamb (2 Samuel 12:1–15), which reveals the truth about David's affair. David is under judgment, but his newborn son will die, not he. David repents and fasts for days, but the boy dies.

This sounds cruel, but, again, we are in the early Old Testament and not the New. Also, some comment that family emotional trauma and guilt can affect the weakest and youngest in a group, causing ill health, failure to thrive and even death. Our actions can have consequences for our families.

Bathsheba has a second son who lives; he is Solomon (from the Hebrew for 'peace'). He was also called Jedidiah, a variant of 'David' meaning 'Loved by Yah'. Solomon was probably his coronation name.

Absalom's Rebellion

In 2 Samuel 13, further dysfunctional aspects of David's family are revealed. His eldest son, Amnon, rapes his half-sister Tamar. Her brother Absalom swears revenge on Amnon, kills him and flees. Absalom is eventually allowed to come back, but David refuses to see him. Absalom, who is very handsome and a great warrior, becomes very popular with the people. He gathers supporters, sets up camp at Hebron and plots to take the throne. His forces march upon Jerusalem and David and his supporters flee. After fierce fighting, Absalom is killed by Joab, much to David's horror. David returns and regains his kingdom.

The Census

The last recorded deed of David's before his death is to hold a census of the people of Israel (2 Samuel 24). He is condemned for this by the prophet Gad and disease comes upon the land. Taking the census showed that David was trusting in human resources and not in the protection of the Lord. Trusting in numbers is seen as the opposite of a faith based upon the promises of God and the power of the Spirit.

KEY VERSES

'The Lord does not look at the things man looks at. Man looks at the outward appearance, but the Lord looks at the heart.'

1 Samuel 16:7b

'He is the one who will build a house for my Name, and I will establish the throne of his kingdom for ever. I will be his father, and he shall be my son.'

2 Samuel 7:13–14

JESUS IN THE BOOKS OF SAMUEL

Prefigurations of Christ in the books of Samuel are seen in the following ways:

- ❑ Anointing the future kings with oil prefigured the anointing and choice of Jesus as King of Kings.
- ❑ Jesus is the promised 'son' who will reign for ever on the throne of his father David (2 Samuel 7:13–14).

❑ Jesus is the trusted and true prophet who will speak the Word of God – Samuel, Nathan, Gad and others prefigure him in this way.

QUICK READ

1 SAMUEL

1 Samuel 1–3 – the Birth and Call of Samuel

1 Samuel 6 – the Ark Returns to Israel

1 Samuel 8 – the People Want a King

1 Samuel 16–17 – David is Anointed and Fights Goliath

2 SAMUEL

2 Samuel 2 – David as King in Hebron

2 Samuel 3 – Joab Murders Abner

2 Samuel 5:6–16 – David Captures Jerusalem

2 Samuel 7 – God's Promise to David

2 Samuel 11–12 – David and Bathsheba

2 Samuel 18 – the Death of Absalom

2 Samuel 24 – the Census

1 and 2 Kings

The books of Kings record the reigns of the kings after David. After Solomon's death, the kingdom splits into two – Israel and Judah. The pattern is established that faithful and godly rulers find blessing, but the cruel and idolatrous bring disaster upon the land.

The Succession

In 1 Kings 1–2, David's death approaches and his son Adonijah, supported by Joab, makes moves to secure the throne. David is visited by Nathan the prophet, who hears the king reaffirm his earlier oath that Solomon will succeed him. Nathan then proclaims Solomon as king. Adonijah flees and clings to the horns at the edges of the altar in the tabernacle, an act that is supposed to grant sanctuary to any who has shed blood innocently. Solomon spares Adonijah, but he pursues Joab by sending Benaiah after him. Joab, too, clings to the edges of the altar, but is struck down in situ, as Joab had deliberately assassinated rivals. Adonijah does not give up, though, and seeks to wed Abishag, the final wife of David, which would have given him a strong claim to be king. Solomon finally loses patience and has him killed.

Wisdom?

Solomon is honoured as the wisest man alive (see 1 Kings 4:29–34), is visited by the Queen of Sheba, and settles the classic dispute between the two women who claim to be the mother of a child (1 Kings 3:16–28). He writes Psalms and Proverbs, but his wisdom as a ruler and spiritually is not so great. He treats the northern tribes of Israel harshly and forces them to build the Temple. He marries 1,000 wives (many to make political treaties) and begins to worship their foreign gods (see 1 Kings 11:5).

The Temple

Solomon takes seven years to build the first Temple in Jerusalem, and a further thirteen years to build a new palace for himself (see 1 Kings chapters 5–7). At the dedication of the Temple, when the ark is brought in, a cloud and bright light fill the place as in the tabernacle in the days of Moses. The priests cannot minister as the holy presence is so strong.

The Split

A rebellion starts over Solomon's treatment of the other tribes, his many wives and the foreign gods (see 1 Kings 11:14–40). This is led by Jeroboam. When Solomon dies, his son Rehoboam becomes king. He is asked to promise that he will treat all the tribes fairly, but in an attempt to appear strong, he states that he will be far harder than his father! The split is inevitable, with the northern kingdom of Israel setting up its capital in Samaria and Judah, to the south, keeping Jerusalem as its capital.

Samaria set up a rival temple cult, and had various altars and sacred sites to rival the Jerusalem Temple. In Samaria, the presence of God was thought to rest upon a base made of two golden calves – the bull was a common Semitic symbol of strength and divinity. There were 17 kings of Israel and 17 of Judah before both nations fell to enemy forces.

Idols and Old Ways

Some rulers set up Asherah poles (fertility symbols representing the goddess Asherah, a female consort of the nature god Ba'al) (see 1 Kings 14:15). Ba'al worship becomes widespread in sacred sites on hills known as 'the high places'.

Ba'al was the force of nature personified; many mixed his worship with that of Yah. Now that they were no longer nomads but a settled, farming people, they looked to local nature deities, and Temple prostitutes were also introduced. Reforming kings such as Asa, king of Judah (see 1 Kings 15:9–24), destroyed the poles and the idols, rededicating the Temple to the Lord and sacrificing there again.

Ahab and Elijah

The 9th-century BC Ahab of Israel was a powerful ruler who married the daughter of the king of Tyre, Jezebel. He could be ruthless and worshipped Ba'al, taking the lead from his wife.

During his reign the prophet Elijah (meaning 'my God is Yah') was active.

Elijah's cycle of stories forms the core of 1 Kings. His high point is the contest with the prophets of Ba'al on Mount Carmel (1 Kings 18:16–40). They assemble to offer sacrifice and to pray for rain after a long drought. The pagan priests dance and wound themselves to no avail. As Elijah prays, lightning strikes his offering – the first sign of a storm and a break in the weather.

After this, afraid of Jezebel's revenge, he flees into the desert. He appears human and vulnerable, despite the great blessings that come upon him. He hides in a cave and hears the voice of God, not in a mighty noise such as an earthquake, wind, or lightning, but within, as a 'still, small voice' (see 1 Kings 19:1–18). Elijah takes Elisha (meaning 'my God saves') as his disciple, finding him as a young man tending his oxen (see 1 Kings 19:19–21).

The Vineyard

In 1 Kings 21 is the story of Naboth's vineyard. Ahab offers to buy it and is refused. Urged on by Jezebel, he has Naboth killed on trumped-up charges of blasphemy and takes the land. Elijah confronts Ahab in the vineyard, pronouncing God's final judgment upon him and his wife. In a panic, Ahab repents, but it is too late. Ahab is killed by a stray arrow, later, and Jezebel falls to her death (see 2 Kings 9:30–37).

Elijah is Taken to Heaven

The book of 2 Kings begins with Elijah condemning the new king of Israel, Ahaziah, who has consulted Ba'al rather than the Lord. Ahaziah dies suddenly. The elderly Elijah then travels with Elisha and a group of fifty prophets. When the end of Elijah's time nears, Elisha asks for a double portion of Elijah's power, and then a fiery chariot comes and whisks Elijah away. Elijah is translated, body and soul, into God's presence, as Enoch had been generations earlier (see Genesis 5:22–24). (In those days, people thought heaven was up above the sky, rather than on a different plane or in another dimension.)

Elisha's Miracles

A cluster of miracle stories follows. Elisha blesses a poor widow whose small jar of oil amazingly keeps on pouring (2 Kings 4:1–7); he raises a boy back to life (2 Kings 4:8–37); he turns a poisonous stew into something edible (2 Kings 4:38–41); he heals a Syrian commander (2 Kings 5:1–19); and he makes an axe head float (2 Kings 6:1–7). The story of the Syrian commander is particularly powerful.

Elisha also has an angelic vision of the Lord's army on the hills as the Syrian army advances (2 Kings 6:8–23). A bright light blinds them and Elisha leads them straight into his capital city, Samaria, where their sight is restored. They are then released.

It is as though blessing follows Elisha wherever he goes, touching people with light and life. There is a darker side, too, however, as when some youths mock him (2 Kings 2:23–25) and are mauled by bears. This is one of the Old Testament's 'nasty stories', and shows that turning against the blessing of God has dire consequences, as even Jesus admits (see Matthew 12:31–32), but this story is a long time before his day, early in the Old Testament history, and of a different covenant! Things then were rougher and retribution was rapid. Fortunately, Christians believe that mercy reigns in the new covenant.

The Fall of Israel

A series of kings (and one queen) follow who are mainly corrupt and involved in family rivalries. Jehu acts righteously, albeit in a very Old Testament sort of way, by slaughtering Ahab's family, including Jezebel, and as many priests of Ba'al as he can find (2 Kings 9–10). Many of the monarchs worship idols, though, and the kingdom of Israel is completely destroyed in 722–721 BC by Shalmaneser, king of Assyria.

The Assyrians moved entire populations to distant parts of their empire, like a game of human chess. Their records state that 27,290 Israelites were moved, and foreigners brought to the area in their place (see 2 Kings 17:1–41). The Israelite faith died out except around Samaria, but there it was a hybrid form that was never recognized by the rest of the Jews.

Attack on Judah

In 2 Kings chapters 18 and 19 is the story of how the southern kingdom nearly falls to Assyria, too. The army surrounds Jerusalem and King Hezekiah repents and prays to the Lord. The Bible reports that an angel of death killed 185,000 in the enemy camp during the night, and the rest of the troops withdrew.

Assyrian records just comment that Jerusalem was besieged, but give no result, though they, like the Egyptians, never recorded a defeat. The Greek historian Herodotus heard a variant version of the story on his travels. In *The Histories*, he wrote that mice came to the enemy camp at night and chewed through all the Assyrians' bow strings! Could there be a link with disease-carrying rodents?

Josiah's Reforms and the Exile

King Josiah follows the precepts in a book of the Law discovered in the Temple. This might have been the whole Torah or a part of it; many scholars think that Deuteronomy was based upon it. Josiah destroys idols and pagan shrines and has the Passover celebrated again – for the first time since Solomon's reign (see 2 Kings 22:1–20)! However, it is understood to be too late to save Judah.

Subsequent kings do not follow Josiah's policies, and King Nebuchadnezzar and the Babylonians cart off the cream of the society to Babylon, only to return later and remove nearly everyone else when rebellion breaks out again in 586 BC. This time the Temple is destroyed and its treasures are looted (see 2 Kings 24–25). (Interestingly, there is no mention of the ark in the list of treasures. No one knows what happened to it – except Indiana Jones!) The Ethiopian Orthodox Church believes that they have it, and a Jewish emigré group might have taken it three centuries ago. No one knows for sure. This period is known as 'the Exile' for obvious reasons. Only a few people of the poorest levels were left behind. The people of Judah were to return in the future, however.

KEY VERSES

'Then a great and powerful wind tore the mountains apart and shattered the rocks before the Lord, but the Lord was not in the wind. After the wind there was an earthquake, but the Lord was not in the earthquake. After the earthquake came a fire, but the Lord was not in the fire. And after the fire came a gentle whisper.'

1 Kings 19:11b–12

'It was because of the Lord's anger that all this happened to Jerusalem and Judah, and in the end he thrust them from his presence.'

2 Kings 24:20

JESUS IN THE BOOKS OF KINGS

In 1 and 2 Kings Jesus is thought to be prefigured by the office of the anointed kings. While they are often far from the ideal, he is the ideal, the perfect servant and Lord. He is also the ideal prophet, the one empowered by the Holy Spirit and who knows the mind of God.

I KINGS

I Kings 1–3 – the Death of David and the Reign of Solomon

I Kings 8 – the Dedication of the Temple

I Kings 12 – the Split between Israel and Judah

I Kings 18–19 – Elijah and Ahab

2 KINGS

2 Kings 2 – Elijah is Taken Up to Heaven

2 Kings 4–5 – Miracles of Elisha

2 Kings 17 – the Fall of Israel

2 Kings 18–19 – Judah is Saved

2 Kings 24–25 – the Fall of Jerusalem

I and 2 Chronicles

The books of Chronicles were written much later than those of Kings, though they cover much of the same material. They were written after the return from Exile, and have a different emphasis.

Three Parts

Chronicles can be separated into three sections:

- ❑ Part One – 1 Chronicles 1–9 – lists of ancient genealogies
- ❑ Part Two – 1 Chronicles 10 – 2 Chronicles 9 – the story of the united monarchy under David and Solomon
- ❑ Part Three – 2 Chronicles 10–36 – the story of Judah in the time of the divided monarchy

The genealogies serve to link the history of the monarchy and Judah back to the creation and to Adam and the patriarchs. Chronicles thus acts as an overview of the Israelite faith and history, going beyond the disaster of the Exile to Babylon and embracing the return to Jerusalem and the land. The fate of the northern kingdom is not dealt with unless it affects the flow of events in Judah.

The Restoration

This took place gradually at the end of the 6th century BC and into the 5th, beginning in 538 BC when King Cyrus of Persia defeated Babylon. He had a tolerant and benevolent policy of restoring the temples and faiths of peoples subject to the Babylonians. It was probably a goodwill gesture, seeking the support of his new subjects, or, perhaps, an attempt to claim the blessing of the High God, no matter what name he was worshipped by. (The Persians followed the Zoroastrian faith by this time, with the belief in one God who was a God of light.) An ancient stone cylinder known as the Cyrus cylinder has survived from Babylon, and sets out his generous policy thus: 'May all the gods whom I have placed within their sanctuaries address a daily prayer in my favour...'

A Second Exodus?

Great hopes had been placed upon the return. Isaiah predicted a new Exodus and a time of great blessings (see Isaiah 35:1–10 and 40:1–11), but this was not to be. Aspects of those oracles have yet to be fulfilled. Small groups returned and the Temple was eventually rebuilt, but this was only a shadow of its former beauty.

The Temple

A central theme of Chronicles is the building of a temple for the Lord. The stories of David and Solomon are retold with this in mind. All Israel was expected to worship there, and David's dynasty was validated by siting itself (and the Temple) in Jerusalem.

Second Chronicles 30:1 – 31:1 tells of Hezekiah's invitation to what remained of the northern tribes to come and worship at the rededicated Temple. A series of passages follows the praise of the Levites, the coming of the ark into Jerusalem and the Temple, and the glorious dedication when the cloud of God's presence fills the place (see 1 Chronicles 15:16; 16:39; 2 Chronicles 5:13; 7:3). Also, the Chronicler stresses the need to worship Yahweh with heart and soul (see 1 Chronicles 22:19).

Praise Brings Victory

King Jehoshaphat sends a band of Levites ahead of his soldiers into battle. They praise God, singing 'Praise the Lord! His love never ends!' God confuses the enemy camp and their forces attack each other. This battle is preceded by a time of prayer, listening and worship. The spiritual lessons from this incident resonate today: praise and worship can dislodge spiritual opposition and darkness (see 2 Chronicles 20:20–23).

The Nations

Yahweh is seen as Lord of the nations, with the activities of Egypt, Babylon and Persia being mentioned (see, for example, material about Shishak of Egypt in 2 Chronicles 12:5–9 and about Cyrus in 36:22–23). Psalm 105 is placed in the saga in 1 Chronicles 16:8–36, and set upon the lips of David. This praises God, who has guided Israel and is owed true worship, as Lord of the nations.

KEY VERSE

'... the land is subject to the Lord and to his people. Now devote your heart and soul to seeking the Lord your God...'

1 Chronicles 22:18b–19a

JESUS IN THE BOOKS OF CHRONICLES

Besides Jesus as the righteous King, the theme of the Temple suggests the need for human beings to build a dwelling fit for the Lord. How can creation welcome the creator and even begin to house his presence? For Christians, Jesus is the fulfilment of this dream. John 1:14 says that in him God's Word 'tabernacled' amongst humanity, a reference to the Old Testament idea of the tabernacle/Temple.

QUICK READ

1 Chronicles 13–15 – David Brings the Ark to Jerusalem
1 Chronicles 16 – Praise to the Lord
2 Chronicles 5 – Solomon has the Temple Dedicated
2 Chronicles 20:20–23 – Jehoshaphat and the Praising Levites
2 Chronicles 29–31 – Hezekiah's Reforms
2 Chronicles 36:22–23 – Cyrus Decrees that the Jews Can Return

Ezra, Nehemiah and Esther

These books cover events during the Persian period. Ezra and Nehemiah are about the gradual return to the holy land; Esther is about life under Persian rule.

EZRA

Ezra was a scribe who came back to Judah in about 458 BC. His book starts off by setting the scene, and some of its chronology is confusing.

Governors and Kings

Sheshbazar returns with a group of exiles, and it is not clear who he is. Some think he was the same person as Zerubabel, who was proclaimed king by the returning Jews. Zerubabel and the priest Joshua set to work rebuilding the altar to offer sacrifices on, and then the Temple itself is rebuilt.

The Trouble with Foreigners...

Chapter 4 offers the disconcerting information that the Jews forbade the local people from helping them even though the natives claimed to have worshipped Yahweh since the Assyrians had settled them there years before. This rejection turns them against the Jews, and there are accounts of opposition to the Temple and to the start of work on rebuilding Jerusalem. Chapter 6 reveals the original decree of Cyrus, and the new Persian king, Darius, recognizes the right of the Jews to carry on building. The Passover is celebrated again.

Ezra finds a community that is deserting the Torah and is intermarrying with the locals. Ezra calls a time of fasting and prayer to seek God in the midst of this spiritual desert. He commands the priests to divorce their foreign wives, as they are leading them astray. This causes ill feelings, and seems to have been an emergency measure to keep purity of faith.

There were earlier traditions in the Torah and the prophetic writings that affirmed foreigners and made them welcome. Some scholars think that the book of Ruth was written at this time (using much older, oral traditions) as a corrective to the zeal of Ezra, reminding people that Ruth, the ancestor of King David, had been a foreigner herself. Of course, she had forsaken her family gods and embraced Yahweh, but could not other foreign wives be given that opportunity, too?

NEHEMIAH

The events in Nehemiah take place 12 years after the events in Ezra. The story begins in Babylon, where Nehemiah is still living and serving the king as his wine-bearer. He is heavy of heart and is given permission to return. Nehemiah finds that Jerusalem's defences are far from finished.

Opposition

Chapters 2–4 relate the opposition from two local officials, Sanballat and Tobiah. Nehemiah appoints 40 men to work on sections of the walls, calls people to prayer and posts watchmen along the defences. Chapters 5–7 reveal more plots, rumours and lies until the walls are rebuilt. The spiritual application of this is that the genuine work of God will be opposed, and attempts to renew faith and to open up to the Spirit will cause a reaction in people who are afraid.

Renewal

Nehemiah has the Torah read aloud to the assembled people. They worship, are moved and repent of their lack of faith and their indifference to the Law. A time of prayer and a commitment to serve Yahweh follow. The principles of tithing, of Temple worship and of providing for the Levite priests (so that they did not have to have a second job) are reinforced. There is then trouble with foreign relatives, who are sent away. This time period was an emergency situation, but it is easy to see how these actions could become overzealous and discriminatory. These impulses could have been tempered by the commands in the Torah to respect the strangers in the community.

ESTHER

Esther is set in the mid-5th century BC in the Persian empire. Many of the details about King Xerxes and life at his court are true to the facts, though some scholars wonder whether the book is more of a parable (a fictional story with a true spiritual meaning) than history. While there is no written evidence of an Esther, Haman or Mordecai in Persian records, such material could one day come to light, and there is no reason why a beautiful Jewess could not have become one of the harem of Xerxes. Some Jews did move east into the Persian cities as others returned to Jerusalem or stayed in Babylon.

Plots

Esther's cousin, Mordecai, discovers a plot against the king. Esther warns the king and it is foiled. Then an order is issued that all should bow low before Haman, one of Xerxes' officials.

Mordecai and the Jewish community refuse, as this is taken to be idolatory. Angry, Haman plots to ethnically cleanse the empire of all Jews, and the date is chosen by casting lots. Mordecai discovers this and pleads with Esther to intercede. Esther appears before the king without being summoned – an action that could have brought instant condemnation upon her – but he accepts her and listens. Haman's plot is foiled, the Jews are protected by royal edict, and Haman is put to death.

The salvation of the people is remembered by the festival of Purim, which comes from the Hebrew word for 'lots'. At this festival, everyone dresses up in fancy dress and the whole book of Esther is read out as people cheer and boo, pantomime style, whenever Mordecai or Haman is mentioned. The funny thing is that God is never mentioned once! His existence, presence and blessing are simply assumed, hidden behind everyday events.

The shadow cast over the Jews in this story is an ominous warning of persecutions to come, especially the terrors of the Holocaust.

KEY VERSES

'O Lord, God of Israel, you are righteous! We are left this day as a remnant. Here we are before you in our guilt, though because of it not one of us can stand in your presence.'

Ezra 9:15

'Remember the instruction you gave your servant Moses, saying, "If you are unfaithful, I will scatter you among the nations, but if you return to me and obey my commands, then even if your exiled people are at the farthest horizon, I will gather them from there and bring them to the place I have chosen as a dwelling for my Name."'

Nehemiah 1:8–9

'Mordecai the Jew was second in rank to King Xerxes, pre-eminent among the Jews, and held in high esteem by his many fellow Jews, because he worked for the good of his people and spoke up for the welfare of all the Jews.'

Esther 10:3

JESUS IN THE BOOKS OF EZRA, NEHEMIAH AND ESTHER

In Ezra, Jesus is prefigured by Ezra as the faithful scribe, teaching the Torah and praying in repentance for the people – Hebrews 4:14–16 reveals Jesus as the high priest who prays for his people. In Nehemiah, Jesus is prefigured as the rebuilder of the walls, the one who surrounds and defends his people. In Esther, Jesus is prefigured by the righteous, honest Jew, Mordecai, standing for what is right even in the face of death threats.

QUICK READ

EZRA

Ezra 3 – Rebuilding the Temple

Ezra 8:15 – 10:17 – the Return of Ezra and the People's Repentance

NEHEMIAH

Nehemiah 1 – Nehemiah's Prayer and Desire

Nehemiah 4 – Some of the Opposition to Rebuilding

Nehemiah 8–9 – the Law is Read and the People Repent

ESTHER

Esther 2 – Esther is Made Queen; Mordecai Discovers the First Plot

Esther 5 – Esther Dares to Approach the King to Plead for the Jews

Esther 9:23–32 – the Feast of Purim and a Summary of the Story

Wisdom

The Wisdom literature is made up of Job, Psalms, Proverbs, Ecclesiastes and the Song of Songs. The Hebrew concept of 'wisdom', *hochma*, is holistic. It is not just intellectual, meaning the right ideas; it is ethical, and regards a way or path to follow. It is practical, about what a person should do, how he or she should live. It is about life skills and any sort of skills – a woodworker could be described as a 'wise man' in their culture. Wisdom is wholesome, and has to do with health, sanity, salvation, humour (light-hearted, relaxing, tension-releasing humour, not nasty mockery) and joy. One verse in Ecclesiastes says that wisdom puts a smile on one's face (Ecclesiastes 8:1). It is a blessing.

The Hebrew Scriptures also personify wisdom, casting the role (metaphorically) as feminine. She was in the beginning with God, before creation came to be, and was an instrument of creation. The New Testament writers saw this as a reference to Jesus, and Paul calls him the Wisdom of God (in the flesh).

The Wisdom writings explore questions of faith and suffering; praise and petition; wise advice; meaning, purpose and depression; and, last but not at all least, love and sex.

Job

The book of Job is a timeless piece of poetry that faces age-old questions about suffering and faith in God.

The Arena of Life

Job is set in the age of the Patriarchs, but it is impossible to date its composition. Some argue that it is based upon a real man, others that it is a parable. Similar poems were written in the ancient world exploring the meaning of life in the face of suffering. The Egyptians produced 'A Dispute over Suicide', for example. This is a dialogue between a man and his soul as he despairs of life:

> 'Behold my name stinks,
> behold more than the stench of fish
> on a summer's day when the sky is hot...'

Job is a righteous man who is not spared suffering. Just why should the good suffer? If we are believers, should we not be blessed and protected? The prologue (Job 1:1 – 2:10) presents a contest, or a bet, between Satan and God. God allows Job to be tested as long as his life is spared. This raises some difficult questions, and the whole book is about the lack of easy answers.

Structure

The book has a prologue and an epilogue (Job 42:7–17). The rest falls into three sections:

- ❑ Job 4–27 – the speeches of Job's three friends, Eliphaz, Bildad and Zophar
- ❑ Job 28 – a discourse on where wisdom comes from
- ❑ Job 29–41 – three monologues, one each by Job, Elihu and God.

The Three Friends

Eliphaz, Bildad and Zophar follow the common wisdom of the day. If a person suffers then they must have sinned (Eastern religions focus on this through their ideas of karma and reincarnation). Job is steadfast that he has not knowingly sinned. He does not know what he has done to deserve this. Even his wife urges him to give up the struggle and to 'curse God and die'. When faced with such pain, it is tempting to give up, to turn one's back on God and embrace the darkness. It is also tempting to try to give people 'pat' answers and to oversimplify great mysteries. To hold on to faith is hard, but to give in is to let the suffering win. Without the light, the darkness is even darker. Faith gives a hope that there is a 'beyond' to all the pain.

Wisdom

The searching genius of human beings can achieve many things, but it cannot find true wisdom. Such understanding, right living and relationship with God is a gift from him. Wisdom dwells with the Creator and is higher than our reason or our abilities to fathom.

Job 28:28 says, 'The fear of the Lord – that is wisdom, and to shun evil is understanding.'

Elihu

Elihu, who thinks that he has an answer that the three friends and Job have ignored, is the raging and impatience of youth. Elihu asks them to consider the mighty works of God, the wonders of nature, the mysteries of the cosmos that we cannot begin to fathom, and wonders what we can say to God. Furthermore, he sees suffering as a refining test of faith and character – God's way of getting our attention. (Noted Christian thinker C.S. Lewis declared that pain is 'God's megaphone'!)

There is some truth in Elihu's ideas, but even the book of Job does not directly declare that God actually sends suffering. Suffering can teach us things, and it can be used by God, but it is not from his hand (see Romans 8:28).

God's Reply

God's reply, which comes from a gathered storm, is to ask Job a series of questions. Can he fathom the mind of God? Can he understand how the world runs or is upheld, day by day? Was he there when the stars were created? Can he tame the leviathan (a symbolic sea monster representing the forces of chaos)? Then Job is given a glimpse of the glory of God, and, in the face of this, he humbles himself and asks no more questions, saying, 'My ears had heard of you but now my eyes have seen you. Therefore I despise myself and repent in dust and ashes' (Job 42:5–6).

Job has been given no answers, only a sense that God is real, despite everything, and is with him. This is the light at the end of the tunnel. Such is the walk of faith. There are many things that we cannot know on this side of the grave.

KEY VERSE

'I know that my Redeemer lives, and that in the end he will stand upon the earth.'

Job 19:25

JESUS IN JOB

Jesus is prefigured in the living Redeemer who will stand upon the earth. Job also prefigures the incarnation and the suffering of God made man. Most Christians feel that all of our questions and arguments about God and suffering must be seen in the light of the cross, as God was there, in the midst of all the pain.

Job 1:1 – 2:10 – the Prologue and the Contest.

Job 28 – Where True Wisdom is to Be Found.

Job 38–41 – God's Reply

Job 42:1–6 – Job's Reply

Psalms

The Psalms are hymns and poems of praise and petition. Some stem from David, some from various other authors. All of life is there, and a range of human emotions. The Greek title was Psalterion, after a stringed instrument, as most were originally set to music. The Hebrew title was simply 'Praises'.

'Of David'

There are three collections of psalms that are headed 'Of David': 3–41; 51–70; and 138–145. This does not necessarily mean that David actually wrote them all. 'Of David' can mean, in the Hebrew, 'concerning', 'of the royal collection', or 'for use by the royal family'. Other psalms are headed 'of the sons of Korah' or 'of Asaph'. Some have no heading. The 150 Psalms are actually 147, but two are repeated (14 and 53), and two separated (9/10 and 42/43). This allowed the collection to be divided into five books, echoing the Torah.

Pilgrims, People and Kings

Besides episodes in the life of David or the people of Israel, the Psalms contain hymns for pilgrims going up to the Temple in Jerusalem and teaching poems that speak to the people and rehearse their salvation history. There are also songs that concern the office and calling of the king. The king is sometimes called 'son' (see Psalm 2). This is not like the pagan ideas of the king being a literal offspring of the gods, but is about spiritual authority and closeness to God. If the monarch was faithful to his call, then God would anoint him greatly with wisdom and grace. The early Christians saw this as prefiguring Jesus as the Son of God. Some believe the mystical Psalm 110 speaks, enigmatically, of the Son being born before the dawn (Psalm 110:3). St Augustine took this as a reference to the eternal Christ, existing before the birth of the sun in the heavens – the divine Light was before the physical light.

Honest Prayer

The Psalms can rarely, if ever, be accused of triumphalism. Some of them betray a deep struggle of faith, a sense of spiritual dryness, of wrestling with pride, of needing to be forgiven. There is anger and frustration and even hatred. There are primitive, ungodly sentiments, such as wanting to smash foreign babies' heads (see Psalm 137:8–9)! These were written by poets, sages and warriors a long time before Jesus, and C.S. Lewis reminds us that they carry the Word of God, sometimes miraculously, through the onslaught of human emotion and limitations.

We can recognize ourselves in these ancient poems, too, and identify with the same struggles. (You mean you've never wished that something terrible would hit your enemy in the face?) The singer Bono, of the band U2, speaks of the Psalms as being like singing the Blues. The authors hit rock bottom, but did not lose faith, and the presence of God picked them up again. There are striking ideas and sentiments, too, verses that seem soaked in the Spirit and alive. It does not matter who wrote them, for God shines through time and time again.

KEY VERSES

'As the deer pants for streams of water, so my soul pants for you, O God. My soul thirsts for God, for the living God. When can I go and meet with God?'

Psalm 42:1–2

JESUS IN THE PSALMS

The royal Psalms are seen as prefiguring the rule and authority of the messiah. Psalm 2 declares that the king is known as 'son'. Psalm 22 is read as a prediction of the Passion; Jesus himself quoted its opening verse when near death, as did Jewish martyrs of his day. Psalm 22:14–18 can be read as a vivid description of crucifixion, along with a reference to casting lots for the victim's clothing (see Matthew 27:35). Jesus is also the ideal shepherd, leading us into life as mentioned in Psalm 23.

QUICK READ

There is no substitute for reading through the Psalms one by one, day by day. Some churches have the practice of selecting some for regular use on a set daily schedule. Some highlights are:

Psalm 1 – the Blessing that Comes from Following God's Way
Psalm 2 – the Coronation of the King
Psalm 22 – a Psalm of Suffering that Relates to the Cross
Psalm 23 – The famous one! 'The Lord is My Shepherd'
Psalm 42 – Thirst for God
Psalm 51 – Repentance and a Desire for Forgiveness after David's Adultery
Psalm 100 – Praise
Psalm 110 – Another Psalm About the Blessings of the King
Psalm 150 – a Clashing, Crashing Hymn of Praise

Proverbs

The book of Proverbs is a collection of short, pithy sayings that should make us think. They concern the quest for Wisdom and how to live in harmony with it, in peace and in blessing.

A Poke in the Heart!

The Hebrew word for 'proverb', *maskil*, can also mean 'oracle' or 'taunt'. The Proverbs are wise sayings that challenge us to think. There are recurring themes, such as seeking for Wisdom; avoiding bad company or being led astray into immorality; and avoiding lethargy and laziness. They are sayings for life on earth, and generally do not contain great spiritual or metaphysical insights into the Beyond or salvation history.

The Wisdom contained in this book is written into life and woven into nature. We reap the consequences if we go against it, whether in health, lifestyle or relationships. The principles are true for all faiths or for those with no faith at all.

Collections

The early chapters are in praise of Wisdom (1:8 – 9:18). Solomon's own proverbs follow (10:1 – 22:16). There is an anonymous collection (22:17 – 24:34), and then Hezekiah's collection (25:1 – 29:27). Collections of Agur (30:1–33) and Lemuel (31:1–9) close the book, preceding the hymn to a good wife (31:10–31). In other words, Solomon did not write them all! Some of the proverbs can also be found in pagan collections of the time, such as in ancient Egypt. This only goes to show that truth is true wherever it is found.

Seek Wisdom!

Wisdom is the personification of God's power. The Old Testament often speaks of God's Wisdom, Word or Spirit as personifications of his presence and power. Wisdom was present at the creation and has been sent into the world to call whom she may (the Hebrew term for 'wisdom' is feminine in gender). Wisdom is a goal for life, a way of life, a path to follow. Decadence was once described as 'the loss of an object or destination in life', so that one does as one pleases and has no clear goal or beliefs. Perhaps Proverbs can thus speak prophetically to our generation.

KEY VERSE

'The fear of the Lord is the beginning of knowledge, but fools despise wisdom and discipline.'

Proverbs 1:7

JESUS IN PROVERBS

Jesus is depicted as Wisdom in the flesh (see 1 Corinthians 1:24, where Jesus is the power and wisdom of God). He was in the beginning with God (see John 1:1). Proverbs 8:22–31 describes the existence of Wisdom from eternity. Wisdom was there before anything was created.

QUICK READ

Proverbs 1 – in Praise of the Way of Wisdom

Proverbs 8 – the Eternal, Pre-existent Nature of Wisdom

Proverbs 10 – the Way of the Wise

Proverbs 31:10–31 – in Praise of a Good Wife

Ecclesiastes and the Song of Songs

Ecclesiastes is a strange book, touching upon the theme of Wisdom, but despairing of any joy or purpose in life until the very close of the book. It is a roller-coaster ride of disillusioned, empty living. The Song of Songs, on the other hand, is a lyrical love poem.

ECCLESIASTES

The Teacher (or Preacher) in Ecclesiastes is identified as a king of Israel – probably Solomon. He starts off by declaring that everything is meaningless (or 'vanity of vanities!' as the old King James version put it). There is 'nothing new under the sun', and he has 'been there, done that'. He has lived a life of pampered luxury, but what is it all really worth? Nothing lasts for ever. Maybe we should just 'eat, drink and be merry, for tomorrow we may die'.

There are tiny glimpses of hope when the author admits that it is better to follow Wisdom than folly (see Ecclesiastes 2:12–14) and that Wisdom can brighten the face (see Ecclesiastes 8:1). Yet he succumbs to gloom again. Life is unfair and unjust – that is the way the world is. Nobody is perfect and no one can know the future.

A Time for Everything

A bright spot can be found in 3:1–17. Here, the author recognizes that there is a season for everything, a time for sowing, a time for reaping. There is a balance and a harmony to life which, as he admits, stems from the Creator. The world is not ultimately empty and pointless. God will be just in the end.

Remember God

The writer cannot let go of a belief in God throughout all the gloom; it pokes through like a beam of light here and there. Finally, in Ecclesiastes 11:7 – 12:14, the author turns back to his Creator. We might not have all the answers, we might go through hard times, but God still is there, just as the sun is really shining even when storm clouds gather.

This is a text by a person who has been through a rough period; it is depressive but bitingly honest. Life can be hard, even when we have faith. Remember God, hold on, the storm will pass.

KEY VERSE

'Fear God and keep his commandments, for this is the whole duty of man.'

Ecclesiastes 12:13

JESUS IN ECCLESIASTES

Christians see Jesus as the figure of Wisdom which is glimpsed and applauded here and there. Jesus is the hope, the shaft of light in dark clouds, the man who went through the darkness of the cross and grave but was raised up.

QUICK READ

Ecclesiastes 1 and 2 – Everything is Meaningless

Ecclesiastes 3:1–17 – for Everything There is a Season

Ecclesiastes 11:7 – 12:14 – Remember God

THE SONG OF SONGS

The Song of Songs, ascribed to Solomon, is a collection of love poems – some of which are quite erotic! It is not always clear who is speaking to whom, and some of the order is confusing, but the sentiments are clear. The description of the bride in Song 4 is very sensual, dripping with bodily imagery and scents. Her two breasts are like fawns, for example. There is joy in the beauty and attraction of her body, and there is nothing wrong with this.

Garden imagery recurs. The secret, walled and perfumed garden was often a metaphor for a woman's body and sexual organs in Near Eastern poetry; to say, 'you are a garden locked up, my sister, my bride; you are a spring enclosed, a sealed fountain' implied virginity. In contrast, Song 5:1 suggests that they have had sex, as do other passages such as 2:16–17.

Fertility Myths?

Some scholars wonder whether there are echoes of ancient fertility myths behind the Song. These contained stories of gods and goddesses weeping for each other as one was carried away to the Underworld. The partner went after them, or wept healing tears that brought them back to life. This was a parable of the seasons, or at least winter and spring.

Certainly there are ideas of longing and absence in the Song, and the idea of 'love strong as death' (see Song 8:6). Cycles of pagan love poems from sacred rituals might have inspired the Song, and they would have been common knowledge in that part of the world. Yet, if these were an influence, then the author has changed so much. There are no deities, only people, and the songs are now about the delight of two people and the pain and longing when they are apart.

God and the Soul?

The rabbis were uneasy that this was just an erotic love poem. They sought an allegorical meaning within it, seeing the king as God and the bride as the soul, or Israel. The church sees it as Christ and the church. There is much that is helpful and true in these allegories. The king coming into the garden is the Holy Spirit entering the believer, and the life that results. The Spirit seals us as his own (see Song 8:6). The soul longs for the presence of God, especially when we have sinned and he seems far away. The 'little foxes' of sin do spoil our spiritual vineyards (see Song 2:15). Perhaps, though, it was just meant to be what it is on the surface, a celebration of the gift of love and sex. They both come from God, anyway.

KEY VERSE

'Let him kiss me with the kisses of his mouth – for your love is more delightful than wine.'

Song 1:2

JESUS IN THE SONG OF SONGS

The love of the king for the bride prefigures that of Christ and the church (Ephesians 5:25–33).

QUICK READ

Songs 1–2 – Love Songs between Bride and King

Song 4 – the Description of the Bride

Song 8 – the Seal on the Heart and Love as Strong as Death

The Prophets

What is a Prophet?

What comes to mind when one pictures a prophet? A mystical, bearded, cloaked figure with glazed eyes? A wizard like Gandalf in *The Lord of the Rings*? Neither is necessarily accurate. The prophets were usually quite ordinary men who felt the touch of the Spirit of God.

The collection of prophetic books in the Old Testament reveals a particular feature of the Hebrew faith. Other ancient peoples had their own version of the inspired go-between whom the gods spoke through. These were the prehistoric shamans, the seers of Ancient Near Eastern cults, or the women at the Greek oracle at Delphi. The common factor was that they went into trance-like states, often induced by wild dancing, by chanting, or by eating herbs.

Prophecy among the Hebrews did not require any of these devices; it simply involved the descent of the Spirit upon a man. It sometimes involved a state of spiritual ecstasy (as in 1 Samuel 19:19–24), but this was from the Spirit, not by working up the necessary emotions. There could be overwhelming experiences of God where the prophet fell face down and was caught up in a vision. This has happened in the recorded lives of holy men and women in the Christian era, too, and can also transpire with some in the church today, such as with the charismatic phenomenon of 'resting in the Spirit'.

Certainly in the Old Testament times, however, these experiences tended to be more unusual and rare. Hebrew prophets had a tremendous sense of God's presence, but this appears to have been more of an internal affair, a moral compulsion and a special knowledge or sense of what should be said. The apostle Paul suggested to early Greek converts that the Spirit of God was not one to put people into 'disorderly' trances, and said that the 'spirits of prophets are subject to the control of prophets' (see 1 Corinthians 14:32–33). Genuine inspiration does not mean being taken over.

Only About the Future?

Prophets did not always speak about the future, and when they did it was often in a very general sense of 'obey God and be blessed, disobey and disaster will strike'. There were particular oracles – prophetic sayings – that went further than this, such as when Jeremiah predicted that Jerusalem would fall to Babylon, and that all the other nations round about would follow suit. This all happened within his lifetime – indeed, within a matter of years. There were more far-reaching predictions, too, such as promises of an age of peace and blessing, and the coming of a special king, the messiah (see Isaiah 9:6–7, or 11:1–9). Most of the time, the prophets were speaking things that the people of the time needed to hear, so that they were more forthtellers than foretellers.

Some prophetic details are therefore obscure, dealing with issues, geography and personalities of a long time ago (hence the need for commentaries!). Nonetheless, many of their insights still speak to us today, and the eternal Word can come through to us from these ancient and long-dead lips.

Major and Minor

There were many prophets who either are not named in the Bible or get only a passing mention. The term 'Major Prophets' refers to those who produced long collections of oracles, such as Isaiah, Jeremiah and Ezekiel. They were active at critical times in the life of ancient Israel. The Minor Prophets, such as Amos, Hosea and Haggai, produced shorter collections.

The prophets spoke what they felt they heard from God in short sayings and long speeches, poems and even in actions (Jeremiah wore an ox's yoke around his neck at one point). These stories and oracles were collected by scribes. Their oracles were usually prefaced by a Hebrew phrase meaning 'An oracle of the Lord', or, as our English Bibles usually put it, 'Thus says the Lord...'

Prophecy in the New Testament

The gift of prophecy carried on after Jesus came. The apostle Paul mentions it as one of the gifts of the Spirit (see 1 Corinthians

12:10), and prophets are mentioned in the Acts of the Apostles (note Agabus in Acts 21:10–11). The book of Revelation is a prophetic book, too, and it specifically states, 'For the testimony of Jesus is the spirit of prophecy' (Revelation 19:10b).

New Testament prophecy reminds us that prophecy is not just about the future, but about encouraging, rebuking, blessing, proclaiming, and perhaps many other things. See, for example, the prophetic words of the risen Jesus to the churches in the first few chapters of Revelation.

Isaiah

Isaiah is a brilliant and penetrating book of prophecies that crystallized aspects of Jewish faith and spoke of the coming Servant and the blessing of the age to come.

One, Two, Three Isaiahs

Isaiah can be divided up into three parts:

1. Chapters 1–39
2. Chapters 40–54
3. Chapters 55–66

These sections have different themes and deal with different ages. Some scholars feel that there are other authors involved besides Isaiah the son of Amoz, who lived in the 8th and 7th centuries BC. This is debatable. However, the styles and concerns of the three parts are different, and it is possible that some of Isaiah's disciples were at work on extending his oracles. There were schools of prophets, and there might have been an Isaiah school. Believers have faith that God spoke, no matter through whom.

Turn!

The key to this part is a call to repentance. God says, 'I reared children and brought them up, but they have rebelled against me. The ox knows his master, the donkey his owner's manger, but Israel does not know, my people do not understand...' (Isaiah 1:2–3). The nation is filled with injustice, empty ritualism, and idolatry. There is hope, though. The Lord says, 'Come, now, let us reason together... Though your sins are like scarlet they shall be as white as snow; though they are red as crimson, they shall be like wool' (Isaiah 1:18). In the Song of the Vineyard in chapter 5, the people of Israel and Judah are like a choice vineyard, carefully cultivated, but producing only bad fruit.

Holy, Holy, Holy...

The call of Isaiah to follow God is described in chapter 6. There the prophet sees a vision of heavenly worship while in the earthly Temple. He hears the thrice-holy hymn, which was taken up in early Christian worship (see also Revelation 4:8). It is a staggering vision of holiness.

Immanuel

Chapter 7 brings the first messianic prophecy in Isaiah, the sign of Immanuel ('God with us'). A virgin will give birth to a child who will bring blessing (the Hebrew might mean 'a virgin' or 'a young woman' – it is open to interpretation though the New Testament also understood it to be 'virgin'). This is followed in chapter 9 with a lyrical description of the blessings of the new age that this child will bring (see Isaiah 9:2–7). Chapter 11 speaks of this child as a branch from the root of Jesse, the father of King David; verses 6–9 give a stunning vision of peace on earth and the knowledge of the Lord filling all things as the waters cover the sea.

Crisis

After a series of oracles for the various surrounding enemy nations, Isaiah turns to the current crisis: Assyria has defeated the northern kingdom and threatens Jerusalem. Chapters 36–39 deal with Hezekiah's reign and God's rescue of the people. This was when thousands of Assyrians were found dead in their camp in the morning. Hezekiah led the people in repentance and God honoured them. The Assyrians had only been given power over nations because God had allowed it; now they could not resist his blessing upon Judah.

PART TWO

Comfort

We shoot forward to the early 6th century BC, when the Jews are in exile in Babylon. They feel defeated and forlorn, and their faith is in tatters. Isaiah prophesies that God has not left them, that he will comfort his people. He is Lord of all the earth, of all the nations, and he can bring to pass what he wills. Chapter 40 ends with an inspiring piece that many take comfort from today: 'Even youths grow tired and weary, and young men stumble and fall; but those who hope in the Lord will renew their strength' (Isaiah 40:30–31).

The Servant

The theme of the Servant of the Lord recurs during this part of Isaiah. The Servant Songs are in Isaiah 42:1–9; 44:1–5; 49:1–7; 52:13 – 53:12. The Servant is nameless in the first and the last references, but he is the nation of Israel in the others. Some feel the Servant might also be Cyrus of Persia, called the Lord's anointed in Isaiah 45:1. Cyrus is also probably meant in Isaiah 41:2, where the Lord asks, 'Who has stirred up one from the east, calling him in righteousness to his service?' (See 2 Chronicles 36:22–23, where Cyrus liberates the Jews from Babylon and allows them to return to their homeland.)

Cyrus was rightfully seen as a great instrument of God's design, but he can hardly fit the spiritual portrait of the enigmatic figure in the other songs. Only one person can, though some scholars have searched for others in vain. Only Jesus fits the descriptions; he identified himself with this figure, and as far back as the first Christians, his followers have agreed.

Thirst!

This section underscores what has gone before, beginning with an invitation to all who thirst. God's grace and blessing are free, but who will receive them? (See Isaiah 55:1–3.) The unfaithful kings are compared with the Servant and castigated, with denunciations against idols and injustice.

Glory!

The book ends with a vision and a hope of future glory: 'Arise, shine, for your light has come...' (Isaiah 60:1). There is a beautiful prophecy in chapter 62 about Israel's new name as she becomes a 'crown of splendour' and a 'royal diadem' in the Lord's hand. No longer cursed and forsaken, the land will be called Hephzibah ('my delight is in her') and Beulah ('married').

KEY VERSE

'We all, like sheep, have gone astray, each of us has turned to his own way; and the Lord has laid on him the iniquity of us all.'

Isaiah 53:6

JESUS IN ISAIAH

Part One prophesies the sign of the child who will bring peace and the glory of the Lord. Part Two speaks of the Servant who is wounded for our transgressions, but who brings peace and redemption. Part Three describes the Lord as coming in majesty, but with garments stained red. This image of God as having waded through the winepress of judgment, but coming to vindicate his people, is seen as a foretelling of Jesus, bleeding for our sins, but expiating God's wrath and bringing us mercy.

Isaiah is seen as being riddled with Jesus! St Augustine taught new converts to read this book before any of the others in the Old Testament.

QUICK READ

Isaiah 6 – the Call of Isaiah
Isaiah 7:14; 9:2–7; 11:1–9 – the Sign of the Child
Isaiah 36–39 – the Assyrians Threaten Jerusalem
Isaiah 42:1–4; 49:1–6; 52:13 – 53:12 – the Nameless Servant
Isaiah 62 – Future Glory and Blessing

Jeremiah and Lamentations

Jeremiah was a prophet who was active from about 622–580 BC. He was the son of a priest who lived just north of Jerusalem. He was active during the reign of five kings, from Josiah to Zedekiah, of which only Josiah was a holy and faithful ruler. Jeremiah's oracles warned that if the people of Judah did not turn back to the Lord, disaster would strike them. They did not listen, and Babylon conquered Jerusalem, destroying the Temple and carrying off many into captivity.

'Lamentations' is a collection of dirge-like poems by an eyewitness (possibly Jeremiah) to the fall of Jerusalem.

I'm Only a Child...

Jeremiah resisted the call to be a prophet, as he was only a young man. Despite this, he was to be given authority and insight beyond his years. In a moving passage, God declares:

> 'Before I formed you in the womb I knew you,
> before you were born I set you apart;
> I appointed you as a prophet to the nations.'
> **Jeremiah 1:5**

The Harlot and the Unfaithful Wife

Judah is called unfaithful. The people have abandoned their first love; the covenant is being ignored, and other gods are being worshipped. Children have even been sacrificed in the Valley of Hinnom. Judah is like an unfaithful wife who has been divorced and has gone with many other lovers. She is defiled, and though no man would go back to her, God will forgive if she repents. Jeremiah chapter 2 poignantly details God's heartbreak and anger.

Foreign Powers

Jeremiah prophesies concerning threats from Egypt and Assyria in the first stage of his ministry, warning about trusting falsely in alliances with these powers. He constantly speaks of a threat from the north, of 'a lion that has come out of its lair'. This is the rising power of Babylon, which overthrew the Assyrians and eventually conquered Egypt.

He spends most of his ministry warning Jerusalem that Babylon is coming and that their rituals cannot save them, for their hearts are all wrong. He prophesies about the surrounding nations such as Edom, Moab, Damascus and Egypt, all of whom would come under Babylonian control as he had warned. Jeremiah lives through the fall of Jerusalem and prophesies hope that there will be a restoration in the future. He tells those taken into exile in Babylon to start businesses and to make homes there, as there will be a restoration in about 70 years!

Dramatic Acts

Jeremiah often performs symbolic gestures to make a spiritual point.

- ❑ He buys a linen belt and ties it around his waist. Then he puts it under rocks for some days and comes to find it again. It is spoiled and unwearable. Thus Judah is spoiled before God (13:1–11).
- ❑ He takes a clay jar and smashes it in front of the leaders of Jerusalem to show that the city and the Temple are both going to be smashed in time (19:1–13).
- ❑ He goes to a potter's shed and watches the man at work,

teaching how God can destroy and start again with his people (18:1–10).

❑ He remains celibate, being instructed by God not to marry, as a sign of loneliness. The people are far from God and will be alone in their time of troubles (16:1–13).

❑ He puts a yoke around his neck as a symbol that the people are going to come under foreign control (27:1–15).

❑ He buys a field when Babylonian soldiers are already taking over the land. This seems a waste of money, but it is a prophetic act, indicating that the land will be theirs again one day (32:1 – 33:11).

Suffering

Jeremiah suffers for his words, as the authorities do not want to hear them. Other prophets prophesy falsely in the Lord's name that the city will be spared. He is mocked, threatened, thrown into prison and put down a well. He only narrowly escapes death on one occasion (another faithful prophet, Uriah, is killed – see 26:20–24). He rants at and curses his attackers at times, showing how real and human he is (see 18:19–23), and when he feels like hiding and not speaking out, he expresses the urges and the drives that a prophet comes under:

> 'But if I say, "I will not mention him
> or speak any more in his name,"

his word is in my heart like a fire,
a fire shut up in my bones.
I am weary of holding it in;
indeed, I cannot.'
Jeremiah 20:9

Hope

Jeremiah sees that though Judah will fall and the Temple will be destroyed, all is not lost. A faithful few will turn to the Lord and return, and this 'faithful remnant' will be all that God needs to raise up a new people and bring blessing to the earth (see, for example, 23:1–4).

This was a painful lesson – that even when something has been blessed and spiritual in the past, if it becomes dead and formal, with a heart turned far from God, then it will be swept aside.

New Covenant

Jeremiah, like Ezekiel, speaks of the coming of a new covenant between God and humanity, a covenant not of slaughtered animals and exterior laws, but of the heart. There will be a spiritual renewal:

'This is the covenant that I will make with the house of Israel after that time,' declares the Lord. 'I will put my law in their minds and write it on their hearts. I will be their God, and they will be my people. No longer will a man teach his neighbour, or a man his brother, saying, "Know the Lord," because they will all know me, from the least of them to the greatest…'

Jeremiah 31:33–34

Lament, Lament!

Lamentations is structured as an acrostic poem for the first four chapters, meaning that each verse begins with a different letter of the Hebrew alphabet. It has been suggested that this was to symbolize completion, that the trials of the people were over. It is grim reading, and expresses honesty in the face of suffering and disillusionment. We have seasons when we need to grieve and feel the pain, but there is a flicker of hope (see, for example, 3:22–27).

KEY VERSE

'I will put my law in their minds and write it on their hearts.'

Jeremiah 31:33

JESUS IN JEREMIAH

Apart from the promise of a new covenant, there is a prophecy about the 'righteous Branch':

'The days are coming,' declares the Lord,
'when I will raise up to David a righteous Branch,
a King who will reign wisely
and do what is just and right in the lands…'

Jeremiah 23:5

 In John's vision, the risen Jesus calls himself 'the Root and the Offspring of David' (see Revelation 22:16).

JESUS IN LAMENTATIONS

Jesus is the lamenting prophet, the one who weeps over Jerusalem years later (see Luke 13:34–35).

QUICK READ

Jeremiah 1–2 – Call and Early Oracles

Jeremiah 13 – Linen Belt and Wineskins

Jeremiah 18–19 – the Potter

Jeremiah 23 – the Righteous Branch

Jeremiah 25 – 70 Years of Exile

Jeremiah 31 – Promise of a New Covenant

Lamentations 1 – the Fate of Jerusalem

Lamentations 5 – the Prayer for Restoration

Ezekiel

The book of the prophet Ezekiel is a fascinating, sometimes bizarre collection of oracles and visions which still speaks with great spiritual insight and authority.

Who Was He, and When?

Ezekiel was a priest of the Temple who was sent into exile (either in 597 BC or 586 BC). He spoke to those who were about to go into exile when Jerusalem fell, and prophesied about the redemption to come, the future hope and the promises of God. He gave a series of oracles, but he also had a string of visions which spoke of profound spiritual truths. He, like Jeremiah, was called to act out some strange rituals to make a point, a divine form of street theatre.

The Call

His call to prophecy begins by a river, when, as he says, 'the heavens were opened and I saw visions of God' (Ezekiel 1:1). Ezekiel 1:4–28 gives the first vision of a cloud flashing with lightning, but surrounded by brilliant light. Within this is a fire, and in the fire he sees heavenly beings with animal and human faces, with wheels beside them that intersect. Above them is a throne of glowing sapphire supporting a fiery man, and a sound like roaring waves is all around. Ezekiel says of the man, 'This was the appearance of the likeness of the glory of the Lord. When I saw it, I fell face down, and I heard the voice of one speaking' (Ezekiel 1:28b). The voice gives him his mission: he is to go to the rebellious people of Judah and call them back to the Lord. His commission is on a scroll, and in the vision, he has to eat the scroll (see Ezekiel 2:1–10).

The vision uses symbol upon symbol to speak of divinity,

 purity, the holy, the eternal, and the angels who are high above this physical realm and who move wherever the Lord moves.

Did He Actually See God?

If God is spirit and beyond human form, then Ezekiel could not see him. If God is not an object within the universe but a living power throughout and beyond all of it, then he has no form. Ezekiel saw a vision, a cluster of dream-like symbols. The Bible tells us he saw 'the appearance of the likeness of the glory of the Lord' and not the actual Lord himself. He is beyond human ken.

Street Theatre

Ezekiel lies beside a brick for over a year (390 days on his left side, 40 on his right). On the brick is a picture representing Jerusalem. He is ordered to eat barley cakes cooked over dried human excrement, but as he shows disgust, the Lord allows him to use cow dung instead. This represents the siege of Jerusalem and the awful conditions that people will have to endure (see Ezekiel 4:1–17).

He has to cut off most of his hair, with the few remaining strands representing the remnant of the people who will be left (see Ezekiel 5:1–12). Another time, he digs a hole in the wall of his house and leaves by night with a bag he has packed. Many watch him but ignore this as another eccentric prank. He tells them that their king will try to leave by stealth, too (see Ezekiel 12:1–12).

When his wife dies, he is told to dress normally and not to eat the food of mourners. People are stunned, but this is to be their fate. They will lose their hearts' desires and will have no chance for mourning (see Ezekiel 24:15–27).

The Glory Departs

In Ezekiel 10, Ezekiel sees the heavenly creatures and the wheels again, but this time the glory of the Lord leaves the Temple and rises above them, leaving with them in tow. This is preceded by visions of idolatry within the Temple and the worship of foreign deities. God's presence could not remain.

Bones

Ezekiel's vision of the valley of dry bones (see Ezekiel 37:1–14) marks a turning point in his oracles. He is speaking of restoration now, and not just about coming judgment. The Spirit blows upon the bones and, stage by stage, they take on sinews and flesh and then life. Though this passage primarily symbolizes the resurrection of the nation after the Exile, many Jews saw a deeper hope of individual resurrection after death in it. Remains of Jewish martyrs from the 1st century AD, for example, have been found with parchments of this passage about them. Just prior to this vision, Ezekiel had expressed the hope of a new covenant (see also Jeremiah 31:33–34) in chapter 36:24–31 – a new heart, the Spirit within people.

The New Temple

The last chapters deal with a vision of an ideal, new temple – a temple that would never be physically built. This was how the temple should be, and a river flows from within it out to the nations bringing healing and blessing. Ezekiel 47 presents the vision of this river, and the prophet is called to walk into it. At first he is up to his ankles, then his knees, and then he has to swim for it! It is seen as a vivid picture of life in the Spirit, as believers are called to move deeper in and allow God to fill them more and more.

KEY VERSES

'I will give you a new heart and put a new spirit in you; I will remove from you your heart of stone and give you a heart of flesh. And I will put my Spirit in you and move you to follow my decrees and be careful to keep my laws.'

Ezekiel 36:26–27

JESUS IN EZEKIEL

Some see the pre-incarnate Son in the figure of the man within the fire and the glory on the throne in Ezekiel's vision. The promise of the new covenant and the river flowing from the temple also appear to speak of Jesus, as the new and perfect Temple in person and from whom the blessing of the Spirit flowed.

QUICK READ

Ezekiel 1–2 – the Call and Vision of the Heavenly Beings and the Wheels

Ezekiel 4 – Lying Before the Brick and the Dung

Ezekiel 37 – the Valley of Dry Bones
Ezekiel 47 – the River from the Temple

Daniel

The book of Daniel is a combination of narratives set in Babylon and picturesque, highly symbolic oracles. Huge debates rage about when it was written down – the 6th century BC or the 2nd century BC.

When?

Daniel was not included in the books of the prophets in the Hebrew Bible. It was placed in a section called 'the Writings' which included the Chronicles, Psalms and other Wisdom books. There is evidence that it was held in high regard as scripture by the 2nd century BC. It is set in Babylon in the 6th century BC and follows the reigns of three kings, Nebuchadnezzar, Belshazzar and Darius. Some scholars think that it was written at that time, and others place it much later on, using old folk memories and stories about Daniel the wise man. They think that it might have been put together in the 2nd century BC when a ruthless Syrian king, Antiochus IV, controlled Judea, and many of the old stories of standing up to tyrants would have resonated afresh. We do not know, but at least some of its stories could go back to ancient times, no matter when it was actually written down.

Two Parts

Daniel chapters 1–6 are a series of stories set in Babylon involving Daniel and his companions, and 7–12 are a series of enigmatic visions and oracles written in a style known as apocalyptic. This latter section is also written in Aramaic, not Hebrew – a later language of the Jews when they were under Persian influence. The apocalyptic style has vivid visual elements, lots of symbols, rulers and nations symbolized as animals, and earth-shaking imagery. There are also cryptic clues and mystical number games. Many scholars see this as a later style of writing, from the 2nd century BC onwards, but traces of it are present earlier, also. The dating debates rage on!

Adventures in Babylon

Daniel and his companions are taken into exile by Nebuchadnezzar. They are placed in royal service and trained at court. Daniel is given a Babylonian name which is Belteshazzar, utilizing the name of 'Bel,' an Ancient Near Eastern deity. They refuse the rich and unkosher foods and wine that are laid out before them, preferring a simpler vegetarian diet with water. Not surprisingly, they are healthier for it! In chapter 2, Daniel comes to fame when he alone has knowledge of what the king has dreamed, and what its interpretation is. The court astrologers are dumbfounded.

Chapter 3 details an attempt to make people worship a golden image of Nebuchadnezzar. Three of Daniel's companions refuse to bow before it, and they are bound and thrown into a fiery furnace. Within the fire, they are unharmed, and what looks like a fourth man walks with them.

This section ends with Daniel being thrown to the lions for daring to pray to his God (see Daniel 6). The presence of God is so strong in him that the lions grow calm and harmless. Stories abound among Christians of wild animals becoming tame and docile in the presence of saints. St Francis was said to have tamed a wolf; maybe animals have a sensitivity to the spiritual that we do not understand.

The Dreams and the Hand

Daniel interprets two dreams of Nebuchadnezzar:

The Statue

The king dreams of a huge statue with a head of gold, chest and arms of silver, belly and thighs of bronze, legs of iron, and the feet partly of iron and partly of clay. A rock, not cut by human hands, strikes the feet and smashes the statue. The rock fills the whole earth.

The metals symbolize different kingdoms and empires, and can be interpreted as:

- ❑ Gold = Babylon
- ❑ Silver = Persia
- ❑ Bronze = Greece
- ❑ Iron = Rome
- ❑ Iron/clay = late Roman empire, which did divide into east and west

The rock is the kingdom of God. If this was from the 6th century BC it is amazing, predicting the Persians, Greeks and Romans. Even if it was composed (at least in part) in the 2nd century BC, it predicted both the rise of Rome and the coming of the messiah. That is still astonishingly accurate.

The Tree

The king sees a huge fruit tree under which animals and people shelter. A heavenly being orders it to be cut down, and its stump is to live in the fields with the wild beasts. Daniel interprets this as a sign that madness is to come upon the king and that he will eat grass like the cattle, but his kingdom will be restored if he turns to the Lord. He does in fact go mad, acting like one of the cattle, his hair long and his nails hard like claws.

This fits a rare mental illness called boanthropy, where people act like cattle. Interestingly, there are references to an illness towards the end of Nebuchadnezzar's reign by ancient authors, as well as an inscription from Babylon which declared that the king lost interest in the city and all his works for four years.

Though it is not a dream, there is also a moving hand whose writing Daniel interprets. Daniel 5 describes a party held by Belshazzar, grandson of Nebuchadnezzar. The hand writes the words 'MENE, MENE, TEKEL, PARSIN' on the wall. Daniel explains that these mean 'Numbered', 'Weighed' and 'Divided'. The days of the king's reign are numbered, his life has been weighed and found wanting, and his kingdom is to go to the Medes and the Persians. (These two groups were later known just as 'Persia'). Darius the Mede is said to take the kingdom, but, in actuality, it was Cyrus. King Darius came one after him. Was this a mix-up, or was Cyrus the same man, also using the name 'Darius'? Was 'the Mede' another altogether, possibly the governor Gubaru whom Cyrus placed in charge of Babylon? We do not know.

The Strange Visions

The apocalyptic sections of Daniel contain three different visions of four beasts and the son of man; a ram and a goat; and a man.

- ❑ The four beasts are a lion, a bear, a leopard and a fierce creature with iron teeth and ten horns. These could be akin to the statue, being Babylon, Persia, Greece and Rome, with the Roman emperors as its horns. The Ancient of Days (God) winds up history and Daniel sees 'one like a son of man' (that is, looking like a human being) who comes on the clouds and is given all authority (see Daniel 7:2–14).

❑ The ram and the goat are said to represent Persia and Greece. The goat has four horns, and one of the horns dares to act like a god and demand sacrifices (a reference to Antiochus IV, who set up an idol in the Temple and tried to wipe out the Jewish faith)(see Daniel 8:1–12).

❑ The vision of a man found in Daniel 10 is of an angelic being who had tried to come to Daniel but had been hindered by 'the Prince of Persia' (a demonic force?) until Michael had come to his aid. The role of the archangel Michael was becoming more defined in Judaism at this time and he is depicted as struggling against evil. This suggests that spiritual forces and battles go on behind the scenes. This has been hinted at much earlier, as with Elisha (2 Kings 6:15–17), and Paul picks this up (see Ephesians 6:10–12).

Resurrection

Daniel 12:1–3 reveals a clear belief in resurrection which has been dawning and growing as the Old Testament progresses:

> 'Multitudes who sleep in the dust of the earth will awake: some to everlasting life, others to shame and everlasting contempt.'
>
> **Daniel 12:2**

Whenever this text was written down, the strong, uncompromising belief in resurrection would have brought hope and comfort to

many who were undergoing great persecution under Antiochus IV.
It is not hard to see why this text was so revered in that age.

KEY VERSES

'In my vision at night I looked, and there before me was one like a son of man, coming with the clouds of heaven. He approached the Ancient of Days and was led into his presence. He was given authority, glory, and sovereign power; all peoples, nations and men of every language worshipped him.'

Daniel 7:13–14

JESUS IN DANIEL

Some see the fourth man in the fiery furnace (Daniel 3:25) as an angel, some as the pre-existent Son. Jesus is clearly predicted in Daniel 7:13–14 with the vision of the 'one like a son of man'. His coming and kingdom are there, too, in the vision of the statue which the rock strikes.

QUICK READ

Daniel 1 – the Arrival in the Royal Court and the Special Diet

Daniel 2 – the Dream of the Statue

Daniel 3 – the Fiery Furnace

Daniel 6 – the Lions

Daniel 7:2–14 – the Four Beasts and the Son of Man

Daniel 12:1–4 – Resurrection

The Minor Prophets – Part One

The 'Minor Prophets' are a collection of short writings covering the period from before the fall of Israel and up to the time of the restoration under Cyrus.

Hosea

Hosea acted out his call to the idolatrous Israelites by marrying a harlot.

The Faithless Wife

Hosea prophesied in the latter half of the 8th century BC, before the fall of Samaria. He marries a prostitute, Gomer, by God's command. Their children are called symbolic names – 'God Scatters', 'No Mercy' and 'Not My People'. Remembering how people treated the meaning of names then, this would have been a powerful damning of the northern nation of Israel. Gomer leaves him and he pursues her, taking her back. Israel is likewise denounced for leaving the Lord but she, too, is called back, for there is mercy and restoration if she returns. There is a moving passage in Hosea 11:1–4 which describes how God tenderly led Israel out of Egypt only to be rejected.

KEY VERSES

'I will heal their waywardness and love them freely, for my anger has turned away from them. I will be like the dew to Israel; he will blossom like a lily…'

Hosea 14:4–5

JESUS IN HOSEA

Jesus is like the faithful husband calling his bride to himself (see Ephesians 5:25–33). Matthew's Gospel also saw an echo of Jesus' descent into Egypt as an infant in the reference to Israel as the 'son' in Hosea 11:1 (see Matthew 2:13–15).

QUICK READ

Hosea 1, 3 – Hosea's Marriage and Gomer's Faithlessness

Hosea 11 – Israel Called Out of Egypt Like a 'Son'

Hosea 14 – Promises of Blessing

Joel

Joel is a short book of prophecy that was probably written in the 9th century BC after a devastating plague of locusts.

Renew the Covenant

Joel is concerned with getting the people to repent of idol worship and to turn to the Lord. The covenant needs renewing in their hearts, for the land has been cursed. Blessing upon the land was closely associated with blessing upon people in the Old Testament (see Deuteronomy 28). The whole assembly of the people is called together, from the priests to babes in arms. God's promises are firmly offered, including the promise of a future outpouring of the Holy Spirit upon all people and all ages. Joel is one of the first prophets to mention the idea of 'the Day of the Lord'.

KEY VERSE

'I will repay you for the years the locusts have eaten…'

Joel 2:25a

JESUS IN JOEL

Jesus is the one who will pour out the blessings of the Spirit in the new covenant. After the Day of Pentecost, the apostles pointed to Joel 2:28–32 as a prediction of this event.

QUICK READ

Joel 2:12–18 – Call to Repentance

Joel 2:28–32 – Promise of the Spirit

Amos

Amos was a prophet who had been a shepherd in Judah. He crossed the border to prophesy in the northern kingdom in the mid-8th century BC, before Samaria fell to Assyria.

Oracles Against the Nations

Amos 1–2 presents a series of oracles against the surrounding nations and ends with ones for Israel and Judah. He calls the separated people to repentance for their idolatry and their injustice. Being an Israelite or a Judean is not enough, he says. He attacks ritualism and religious hypocrisy (see Amos 5:21–24). His appeal for the poor fits with archaeological knowledge of that period – there were poor, small dwellings and expensive ones for the rich, with little in between. Amos also uses the term 'Day of the Lord', turning this on its head for his Israelite listeners. They thought that it would vindicate them; only, says Amos, if their hearts are right with God.

Visions

Amos has two visions, one of a plumb line and one of a basket of ripe fruit. The plumb line (Amos 7:7–9) shows that the Lord is going to knock down and rebuild the nation. They are being measured up to see what was in line, being readied for judgment. The ripe fruit (Amos 8:1–2) suggests that the time is ripe for judgment. God's patience is coming to an end.

Other Nations and God's Care?

Amos 9:7 contains the amazing idea that the Lord is over all the nations (an early expression of this) and that he has been behind various movements of peoples, using the same Hebrew word as 'exodus' of them:

> 'Did I not bring Israel up from Egypt,
> the Philistines from Caphtor
> and the Arameans from Kir?'

There is a grace and a mystery about God's presence and purposes outside the covenant (old or new). Where there is not explicit faith in him, we cannot say that he is necessarily absent.

KEY VERSE

'But let justice roll on like a river, righteousness like a never-failing stream!'

Amos 5:24

JESUS IN AMOS

Christians believe Jesus was the perfect Israelite, being the righteousness of God. His justice and mercy were seen in his inclusion of the social and religious outcasts of his day. He is also seen as the fulfilment of the promise of Amos 9:11, 'In that day I will restore David's fallen tent…' and the hope that Israel would be planted again, never to be uprooted (Amos 9:15).

QUICK READ

Amos 2:4–16 – Oracles Against Judah and Israel
Amos 5:21–27 – Religious Hypocrisy Denounced
Amos 7–8 – Visions of Plumb Line and Fruit
Amos 9:11–15 – Future Blessings

Obadiah

A one-chapter book of prophecy! We are not sure when this was written.

Who, What and When?

Obadiah prophesies against Edom, for that nation had stood by and had not aided Israel when an invader (Babylon?) had appeared. Scholars note a similarity between Obadiah verses 1–9 and Jeremiah 49:7–22. He uses the idea of the 'Day of the Lord', warning all nations that this will come.

KEY VERSE

'The day of the Lord is near for all nations. As you have done, it will be done to you; your deeds will return upon your own head.'

Obadiah verse 15

JESUS IN OBADIAH

Jesus is the one in whom deliverance is found, just as it was in Mount Zion (Obadiah verse 17). Jesus is the one who is mighty to save.

QUICK READ

Obadiah verses 8–12 – the Sin of Edom's Standing By

Obadiah verses15–18 – the Day of the Lord

Jonah

Jonah's book of prophecy is unusual as it is mainly composed of narrative. He only prophesies one thing: that in 40 days' time, Nineveh will be destroyed.

Run Away!

Jonah's story is of a reluctant prophet who does not want to go to the Assyrian capital, Nineveh, despite being called to 'preach against it' by the Lord. He wants a peaceful, easy life and takes to the sea instead, planning to travel to Tarshish, Spain. This was then the furthermost point of the known world. In other words, Jonah is getting as far away as possible, but God catches up with him. During a great storm, the sailors draw lots to see who is at fault for the gods' anger. It is Jonah, and he is tipped overboard. God, in his mercy, spares Jonah; a 'big fish' (that is what the Hebrew actually says) swallows him and he is alive inside it for three days and three nights. Desperate and repentant, Jonah prays to his Lord, and the fish spews him out onto dry land.

Sometimes people try to ignore the call of God, and might actually turn directly against it. Believers agree that we can't run away from his Word for ever. For a believer, there is no peace, no rest, until we face it.

Interestingly, Jonah managed to sleep during the storm. Does that not suggest a deep-down sense that God was with him no matter what? A similar scene is found in Mark 4:35–41, where Jesus sleeps during a storm.

How Dare God Forgive!

When Jonah gets to Nineveh, he is stunned to find that the Assyrians heed his message and repent. Jonah is angry that God has forgiven his enemy. In response, a vine grows up to give shelter to Jonah; the next day, it withers and Jonah is scorched by the sun. God speaks to the prophet, reminding him that God will have mercy on whom he wills, just as he had been merciful to Jonah by giving him shade. The Lord asks, 'But Nineveh has more than a hundred and twenty thousand people who cannot tell their right hand from their left, and many cattle as well. Should I not be concerned about that great city?' (Jonah 4:11).

Fact or Fiction?

Scholars disagree about whether the book is a parable or a historical account. Regardless, it teaches a lesson – the need for obedience and the mercy of God (even upon one's enemies!). This lesson is true whether it is a made-up story or not.

Certainly the 'big fish' element makes some doubt, but it has been suggested that a species of whale such as the sperm whale would be able to swallow a person whole, and that if he/she reached the laryngeal pouch, then there would be enough air supply. There are a few stories about people actually surviving situations like this, such as one in 1891 when a sailor was said to have emerged unharmed from a sperm whale except for skin damage. The trouble is that these are hearsay and there is no modern account that can be corroborated.

Neither do historians know of any great change of heart by the Assyrians, but there is much that is not recorded or has been lost. Additionally, their repentance might not have lasted. In any case, Jonah is mentioned as being a prophet from Gath Hepher in 2 Kings 14:25. This would place him after Elijah and Elisha, late in the 8th century BC, prior to the fall of Nineveh in 612 BC. The dates thus would all fit perfectly.

KEY VERSE

'But I, with a song of thanksgiving, will sacrifice to you. What I have vowed I will make good. Salvation comes from the Lord.'

Jonah 2:9

JESUS IN JONAH

Jesus himself used Jonah as a type of himself (see Matthew 12:39-41 and 'the sign of Jonah'). Just as Jonah was in the whale's belly for three days and then released, so Jesus was to be in the earth three days and then rise again.

QUICK READ

Jonah 1 – Jonah Flees

Jonah 2:10 – 3:5 – Jonah in Nineveh

Jonah 4 – the Vine and Jonah's Anger

The Minor Prophets – Part Two

Micah

Micah lived from the 8th century BC to the early 7th century BC. He was a contemporary of Isaiah and prophesied under three kings, Jotham, Ahaz and Hezekiah.

Origins from of Old

Micah was concerned with the threat of Assyria, with Samaria falling to the invaders in 721 BC. He warned Judah that this would be their fate unless they repented. There are many vivid passages about the Lord's power and judgment, but two passages in particular stand out for posterity. The first, in Micah 4:1–5, is about the 'mountain of the Lord' and the peace that will come to all nations ('they will beat their swords into ploughshares…' – an oracle also present in Isaiah 2:1–5). The second is an oracle about Bethlehem, an insignificant village but for the fact that it was the ancestral homeland of King David. Micah 5:2 speaks of a coming king from Bethlehem with the enigmatic phrase 'whose origins are from of old, from ancient times'.

KEY VERSE

'He has showed you, O man, what is good. And what does the Lord require of you? To act justly and to love mercy and to walk humbly with your God.'

Micah 6:8

JESUS IN MICAH

Jesus is held to be the ruler foretold in Micah 5:2 who will hail from Bethlehem and whose 'origins are from of old'.

QUICK READ

Micah 4:1–5 – the Mountain of the Lord and Peace on Earth

Micah 5:2 – the Bethlehem Oracle

Micah 7:14–20 – Blessings and Hopes

Nahum

Nahum lived in the 7th century BC and prophesied the fall of Nineveh (which happened in 612 BC).

Nahum speaks of the Lord's holiness and judgment: 'He rebukes the sea and dries it up; he makes all the rivers run dry'

(Nahum 1:4). Nineveh is now beyond help and they have a fatal wound: 'I will prepare your grave, for you are vile' (Nahum 1:14). The prophet refers to the fall of Thebes (in 663 BC) in Nahum 3:8, asking Nineveh if she is any better than that great city. From Jonah, we heard that Nineveh had been given a chance for mercy, but this had finally been spurned.

KEY VERSE

'The Lord is slow to anger and great in power; the Lord will not leave the guilty unpunished. His way is in the whirlwind and the storm, and clouds are the dust of his feet.'

Nahum 1:3

JESUS IN NAHUM

Jesus is seen in the righteousness of God and the avenging of God's people. Jesus, who came with mercy and service, will return in power and glory.

QUICK READ

Nahum 1:2–8 – the Lord's Holiness and Justice

Nahum 3:8–13 – Thebes Compared with Nineveh

Nahum 3:18–19 – Final Words Against Nineveh

Habakkuk

Habakkuk was a contemporary of Jeremiah who also prophesied the fall of Jerusalem in 597 BC.

Talk, Talk

Habakkuk is unusual in that it is set in dialogue form (as is Job). The prophet issues two complaints and then records the Lord's replies. The final chapter is a long prayer by the prophet that ends in a classic section of praise even when circumstances are hard.

KEY VERSE

'Look at the nations and watch – and be utterly amazed. For I am going to do something in your days that you would not believe, even if you were told.'

Habakkuk 1:5

JESUS IN HABAKKUK

Jesus is seen as being prefigured in the image of 'God my Saviour' who will save his people despite all that is to come upon them. He is the strength of the prophet who enables him 'to go on the heights' (Habakkuk 3:19). Through the cross, resurrection and the gift of the Holy Spirit, Christians have faith that their souls can ascend 'on the heights', growing close to God.

QUICK READ

Habakkuk 1:1–7 – the Prophet Cries Out for Justice, and the Lord Says that the Babylonians Are Coming

Habakkuk 2:18–20 – Worthless Idols

Habakkuk 3:16–19 – Praise in Hard Times

Zephaniah

Zephaniah was a member of the royal family in the days of King Josiah (640–609 BC). The oracles concern the early days of the reign as described in 2 Kings 22:1 – 23:30.

Judgment is Coming

Zephaniah seeks to turn the people from idol worship and warns of the coming 'Day of the Lord', which means that Judah will also be judged.

KEY VERSE

'At that time I will deal with all who oppressed you; I will rescue the lame and gather those who have been scattered. I will give them praise and honour in every land where they were put to shame.'

Zephaniah 3:19

JESUS IN ZEPHANIAH

Jesus is seen as 'the Lord... mighty to save' (see Zephaniah 3:17). The name 'Jesus' means, after all, 'the Lord saves'.

QUICK READ

Zephaniah 1:4–18 – Oracles Against Judah and Ba'al Worship
Zephaniah 3:14–20 – Hope in God as Saviour

Haggai

Haggai was one of the returning exiles from Babylon. He wrote in the second year of Darius (520 BC).

The New Temple's Glory

Haggai surveys the situation in Judah 20 years after the Jews' return. Zerubbabel is governor of Judah and Joshua is the high priest. Haggai gives the Lord's command to rebuild the ruined Temple; the people are building fine houses for themselves but not for the Lord. Thus, they suffer from a lack of blessings, among them prosperity (see Haggai 1:3–6).

Haggai prophesies that the glory of the new Temple will be greater than that of the old. In fact, it wasn't anywhere like the first one. However, if this oracle is seen to relate to the new covenant and the Body of Christ, then its glory far surpasses that of Solomon's Temple (see Haggai 2:7–9). There are hints of an earth-shaking new beginning, and Zerubbabel is declared to be 'the signet ring' of the Lord, a royal and messianic title.

KEY VERSE

'This is what the Lord Almighty says: "In a little while I will once more shake the heavens and the earth, the sea and the dry land."'

Haggai 2:6

JESUS IN HAGGAI

Jesus is to be the restorer of the heritage of the people of God. He will be the new Temple whose glory far surpasses that of Solomon's. He is to be the signet ring, the royal Son of David's line.

QUICK READ

Haggai 1:1–11 – the Poverty of the People and the Need for a Temple
Haggai 2:6–9, 20–23 – the Shaking of the Heavens and the Signet Ring

Zechariah

Zechariah was a contemporary of Haggai and the son of a priest who had returned from exile. Zechariah is a book of visions and bizarre oracles that has a style rather akin to the apocalyptic style of Daniel.

Visions, Messiahs, and a Shepherd

The first part of the book gives 8 visions, such as the strange riders (Zechariah 1:8–17), the high priest confronting Satan (Zechariah 3:1–10), and lamps and olives (Zechariah 4:1–14). The second part of the book contains oracles about the future and the people of Israel.

Zechariah 6:9–11 describes the crowning of Joshua as the high priest, but verse 12 declares, 'Here is the man whose name is the Branch...' This was a messianic title, i.e. a title of the coming king, but priests and kings were separate entities. This led to speculation that there would be two messiahs, a priestly and a royal one. Jesus is seen in the New Testament as priest and king, combining the two.

Zechariah 11 prophesies the coming of a faithful shepherd after the people have been failed and led astray by poor shepherds. Zechariah 13:7 speaks of the wounding of the shepherd and the sheep scattering, and 13:1 declares that there will be a fountain to cleanse the people of all sin.

KEY VERSE

'On that day a fountain will be opened to the house of David and the inhabitants of Jerusalem, to cleanse them from sin and impurity.'

Zechariah 13:1

JESUS IN ZECHARIAH

There are rich prophetic glimpses of Jesus in Zechariah. He is the fountain that is opened to cleanse from sin; he is the faithful shepherd who is wounded and whose followers flee. He is king and high priest together. Zechariah 11:13, which describes throwing money to the potter, was used by Matthew as a prediction about Judas Iscariot (see Matthew 27:9).

QUICK READ

Zechariah 4 – the Vision of the Lamps
Zechariah 6:9–15 – Joshua Crowned as High Priest
Zechariah 12:10 – 13:9 – the Wounded Shepherd

Malachi

Malachi means 'messenger' and it is thought that he was a contemporary of Ezra and Nehemiah. He addressed the condition of the returning exiles.

The Last of His Line

Malachi castigates the people for empty rituals and for ignoring the needs of the Temple. He sees that a true heart conversion and giving of tithes would bring blessing to the land. He bemoans blemished sacrifices – crippled or diseased animals – as the Torah demanded the best. 'Oh, that one of you would shut the Temple doors, so that you would not light useless fires on my altar,' says Malachi 1:10. Malachi prophesies that a pure offering will be made all over the world (Malachi 1:11).

He urges the people to pay their tithes – 10 per cent of their produce – to the Temple to allow God's service to go on, and says that a blessing would return to them if they did. He also speaks of a messenger who is to come suddenly (see Malachi 3:1 and 4:5–6), saying, 'See, I will send my messenger, who will prepare the way before me.' The messenger is also referred to as Elijah.

Malachi was the last prophet before the appearance of John the Baptist.

KEY VERSE

'But for you who revere my name, the sun of righteousness will rise with healing in its wings.'

Malachi 4:2

JESUS IN MALACHI

Jesus is said to have been predicted in the 'sun of righteousness', and in the pure offering. Malachi 1:11 refers to spiritual sacrifice from the lips of members of the Body of Christ, and many in the early church also saw a prediction of the eucharist in this. The 'messenger' and Elijah prefigured John the Baptist.

QUICK READ

Malachi 1:6–11 – Blemished and Pure Offerings
Malachi 3:1–5 – the Messenger
Malachi 3:6–12 – Giving, Tithes and Blessing
Malachi 4:5–6 – the Coming of Elijah

The Apocrypha

Some Bibles – Catholic and Orthodox translations – have extra books in the Old Testament. This is because the Greek translation of the Old Testament included them, but the Hebrew one did not. The Greek translation might have been begun as early as the middle of the 3rd century BC and was complete by the early 2nd century BC. The Hebrew Scriptures were collected into a recognized canon (a rule, or list of agreed books) much later, after the fall of Jerusalem in AD 70.

The books included in the Greek version – Tobit, Judith, 1 and 2 Maccabees, Wisdom, Ecclesiasticus and Baruch – were written later than the other Old Testament books, in the main. They were generally products of the 2nd century BC, and display later ideas. Some of their historical details are questionable, and they seem to have been written to teach and exhort rather than to present accurate details. The Protestant reformers omitted them because the Hebrew canon had done so. They are not thus regarded by the Protestant Church as scripture, but as devotional literature that is profitable to read.

There is much in these books that is rich and rewarding – ideas that were taken up by early Christianity. The idea of the resurrection of the body is affirmed; we find the ministry of angels and the existence of demons; and much is written about

Wisdom. Some of these texts were used by the New Testament writers. Hebrews 1:3, for example, uses Wisdom 7:25–26 to speak of Jesus. Also in that letter, the reference to 'entertaining angels unawares' (Hebrews 13:2) probably refers to the story of Tobit and the angel Raphael, who disguises himself as a traveller. The end of the list of Old Testament heroes of faith (Hebrews 11:32–39) speaks of those who went out into the deserts – a probable reference to the Maccabees.

There is no new doctrine, except for the fact that references to prayers and sacrifices for the dead and comments on the role of the saints in intercession can be found in 2 Maccabees (see 12:39–45 and 15:12–16). These are issues of contention between Catholic and Reformed Christianity.

TOBIT

Tobit is a moving story about love, marriage, angels and healing. Tobit goes blind after sleeping out in the open on a hot night – bird droppings fill his eyes and infect them. (He finds healing later through the ministrations of Raphael the angel.)

Tobit's son, Tobias, travels to settle business with one of Tobit's acquaintances. He meets a fellow Israelite, a stranger, along the way who tells him to take a fish and use its heart and liver to repel a troublesome demon, and to bring the gall to his father. The stranger turns out to be the angel Raphael, whose name means 'God is healer', and who reveals himself at the end of the story as one of the seven angels who stand before the throne of the Lord. Tobit and his family bow low in terror. Raphael tells them to worship God alone and to give thanks to him.

JUDITH

Judith, meaning 'the Jewess', is about a brave woman of faith, a widow, who risks her life to save her people. Nebuchadnezzar's commander, Holofernes, is sent to teach various subject nations a lesson. The Jewish high priest, Joakim, calls for the people to repent, fast and pray. Eventually, Judith's town of Bethulia is besieged. Judith puts on her finest clothes and jewels and leaves the town.

When Judith is questioned, she claims to be fleeing from her people and says she wishes to give information to Holofernes himself. He is taken by her beauty and brings her to a feast, where he is so smitten that he drinks far too much wine and falls into a deep sleep. She is left alone with him, takes a scimitar, and chops off his head. She secretes this in her food bag and returns to Bethulia. The enemy flees and Judith is fêted.

1 AND 2 MACCABEES

The books of Maccabees are about freedom fighters who resist foreign tyrants and are zealous for the Torah. 1 Maccabees gives a reliable history of the Jewish resistance movement against the Syrian ruler Antiochus Epiphanes, who came to power in 175 BC and tried to bring Greek culture and customs into Judea. He erects an idol in the Temple and forbids the Jews from keeping the sabbath and from sacrificing. Some flee into the hills and preserve the scrolls of the Torah. Mattathias starts the uprising by killing an apostate Jew who is about to sacrifice to a pagan god. The rebels withdraw to the desert and are led by Judas Maccabeus ('the Hammerer'), who defeats Antiochus, rules in Judea from 166–160 BC and even seeks an alliance with Rome and Sparta. Judas cleanses and rededicates the Temple.

The second book of Maccabees retells some of the same story. It is more sermonizing, seeing the persecutions as God's judgment upon the people and a call to bring them back to him.

WISDOM

Wisdom is a book of praise for Wisdom, for the life of virtue and for God's dealings within history. Wisdom (or 'The Wisdom of Solomon' in the Greek text) was probably written in the 1st century BC in Alexandria. Though the author claims to be a king (see 9:7–8), this is a literary device, saying that the author is writing in the wisdom and spirit of Solomon of old – under his patronage, as it were.

Chapters 6–9 explore the mysterious and awesome nature of Wisdom, saying, 'For it is an inexhaustible treasure to men, and those who acquire it win God's friendship' (Wisdom 7:14). The description in Wisdom 7:25–26 was used by the author of Hebrews in the New Testament to speak of Jesus.

ECCLESIASTICUS

Ecclesiasticus was a name given later to this book. It was originally known as The Wisdom of Jesus Ben Sirach. Some of its sayings are used in the Epistle of James in the New Testament.

Ben Sirach lived in the early 2nd century BC and probably wrote on the eve of the Maccabean revolt. He was critical of Greek influence upon his land and faith. Ben Sirach was a pious Jew who extolled traditional virtues and the Torah. He equated Wisdom with the Torah.

Ecclesiasticus has a wonderful hymn of praise to Wisdom in chapter 24, tracing her beginnings from eternity, how she pitched her tent with Jacob, and how she has grown like tall, strong trees and gives off a beautiful fragrance.

BARUCH

Baruch is addressed to the people of Jerusalem from Babylon. It contains prayers, Wisdom material and messianic hopes. The book claims to have been written by Baruch, the scribe of the prophet Jeremiah. The text was written in Hebrew originally and is hard to date. Many place it in the 2nd century BC. We do not know if any tradition had come from Baruch himself, but this is possible.

A Wisdom poem fills chapters 3:9 – 4:4, and says that Wisdom is the way to life, a mystery that is grasped only by God himself. Just like Ben Sirach, Baruch equates Wisdom with the Torah, claiming, 'those who keep her live, those who desert her die' (Baruch 4:1).

Introduction to the Gospels

A 'gospel' is a unique type of literature. 'Gospel' means 'good news', and the four books about Jesus are good news books. They are not just historical accounts of his life and teaching – though they include those. They are proclamations, announcements of the good news that the saviour has come. To an extent, they explain and analyse and challenge, as well as relating old stories and sayings. There is nothing quite like them in the literature of the ancient world. They not only tell the story of a long-dead hero, but proclaim him as risen and alive today. Christianity does not live on nostalgia; it celebrates an eternal presence.

Matthew, Mark and Luke

The first three Gospels follow a similar pattern. Mark was probably written first and is the shortest. Early church tradition claims that Mark was a companion of the apostle Peter. Matthew, one of the twelve disciples, was said to have written the sayings of Jesus in the Hebrew language. It is not clear whether this meant the whole of the Gospel of Matthew or a cluster of traditions that it draws upon. Luke was a travelling companion of

Paul. Matthew and Luke contain huge portions of Mark, but they adapt and add their own material. Some of this is in common – a collection of sayings (and a couple of narratives) that might have formed an early (possibly oral) tradition of Jesus' teaching that was circulating around the first churches.

The pattern that the first three Gospels follow is the outline of the ministry of Jesus as found in the early apostolic preaching as recorded in the book of Acts. See, for example, Peter's sermon to Cornelius in Acts 10:36–41. This has the following scheme:

- ❏ The ministry began in Galilee after Jesus' baptism by John.
- ❏ The ministry involved the power of the Holy Spirit, with healings and exorcisms.
- ❏ Jesus ended his days in Jerusalem, where he was crucified.
- ❏ God raised him on the third day, and the apostles were witnesses to this.

Flicking through Mark, one will see that this is the scheme that he uses, as do Matthew and Luke.

John

The fourth Gospel, John, is somewhat different. John is identified with the 'beloved disciple' in that Gospel, where he is said to be the apostle John. There are some sayings and narratives that parallel those in the other Gospels, but there is much new and original material, too. In John we see that Jesus was active in Galilee, but he also visited Jerusalem at festival times before his final week, healing and teaching. The kinds of healings are as we find in the other Gospels, but there are new stories. Jesus teaches in long, profound speeches rather than the one-liners and parables in the other accounts.

John is often described as the 'spiritual Gospel'. It seems to go deeper, revealing Jesus in all his glory as the incarnate Son of God.

Oral Tradition

Luke tells us that many had tried to write accounts of what Jesus had said and done (Luke 1:1–4). It is likely that there was an oral tradition about Jesus that ran parallel to early writings about him (a hint in an early Christian writer suggests that this carried on for some time, even after the four Gospels were written).

This should not be taken as casting doubt upon the accuracy of the eventually written words. People then were more used to recalling information, as theirs was a less literate society. Traditional societies have strong oral traditions that can be passed down carefully for many years. There are some who are especially trained in this; one rabbi at the time of Jesus declared that 'a well-trained pupil is like a well-plastered cistern'. This was to suggest that pure knowledge could be drawn from such a pupil again and again.

The Passion Narrative

Scholars think that the first attempts at writing out part of the Jesus story were for worship purposes, when the community gathered to share communion and the story of the last supper and the passion were read out.

One main focus for these stories was the connection of Old Testament messianic prophecies to Jesus, as is seen in the similarity between Mark 15:24 and Psalm 22:18 or repeatedly in Matthew's birth narrative. An aspect of this was, of course, the rejection and execution of Jesus by his own nation that was foreshadowed in Isaiah's prophecy of the suffering servant (Isaiah 52:13 – 53:12).

Throughout history the passion narrative has been wrongly used to further the cause of anti-Semitism. Jesus was, in fact, put to death by the Roman authorities, though with the support of the Jewish authorities and a mob that likely had been bribed, threatened, or generally rounded up for their effect on Pontius Pilate. It is probable that they were not a representative group; many in the nation did in fact support Jesus and seem to have been disappointed in his apparent failure.

The point to remember is that many in the nation knew, supported and loved Jesus, despite the views of the religious authorities.

Miracles in the Gospels

Jesus was full of the presence of God. He affected people around him – some positively, some negatively, and some in ways that can only be described as miraculous.

That Jesus was a healer as well as a teacher is attested from early on in the gospel tradition and the preaching of the apostles. There are many healing stories told about him, and it is interesting to speculate on what might lie behind these. There might be psychological cures, where people felt forgiven and released from guilt. There is so much about the power of the mind that we do not understand. There is also a lack of understanding of the power of the Holy Spirit as a force for good.

Whatever people make of the healing miracles, or some of the other types (turning water to wine, walking on water, etc.) that are known as the nature miracles, the two greatest miracles are the incarnation (God becoming man) and the resurrection. Here we are dealing with mysteries and stand on awesome, holy ground. They are spiritual events that defy analysis, ultimately. (For a fuller discussion about miracles, see the appendix at the back of this book.)

Matthew

Matthew is a Gospel with a distinctly Jewish flavour. It is concerned with the Torah and the fulfilment of Jewish prophecy.

Angels and Stars

Matthew begins with a long genealogy tracing the ancestry of Jesus back through David and Abraham. It is tempting to skip this bit, just as a Bible-translating missionary was tempted to do when working with an African tribe. He didn't, and he was glad; the tribe responded warmly, for this Jesus had a history and pedigree, like any other real man, and thus was more readily received.

Matthew adds birth stories of Jesus, which include the vision of the angel to Joseph telling him that God has blessed Mary with the child, and the message that they are to flee into Egypt. The wise men ('magi' in the Greek, meaning all-purpose philosopher, spiritual expert and stargazer of the ancient world) come to find Jesus. The text does not actually say how many there were (there were three gifts, though) and they were not kings! People read meanings into the gifts – gold for a king; frankincense for a god; and myrrh for burial. They might just have been expensive gifts; nonetheless, their symbolism can be edifying.

Various theories try to locate and explain the star. There were strange events at this time recorded by the ancient Babylonians and Chinese. There were comets, supernovas and a conjunction of two planets that would have shone like one, bright star.

We have no record of the slaughter of the innocents in ancient histories, but Herod is described as a ruthless and cruel ruler who would have been capable of such a horrible deed, and Bethlehem was only a small village at the time.

Mary is described as a *parthenos* in the Greek text. Some point out that this need not mean virgin, but can also simply be a 'young woman'. However, its precise meaning has to be decided in ancient texts by its context. Clearly, here, she is a virgin.

The birth narrative uses no fewer than five Old Testament references to show that Jesus is the promised messiah.

The Sermon on the Mount

Matthew collects a cluster of sayings and presents this on a mountain, perhaps trying to show that Jesus is a new Moses, a new Lawgiver (remember Mount Sinai and the Ten Commandments?). Matthew 5:2–12 are very special 'one-liners'. These are known as the nine beatitudes, from the Latin *beatus*, meaning 'happy' or 'blessed'. In them, Jesus reverses the values of the world, seeing the lowly and the poor as blessed. God is close to the humble, and those who weep over their sins and cast themselves upon God's mercy are close to the kingdom. Pride is a barrier that shuts God out.

The other teachings share a common theme: external piety is not enough, for we need to have a change of heart. Prayer, for example, is to be in a secret place (see Matthew 6:6) and not in public. The sermon also contains a version of the ethical 'Golden Rule' which is found in various faiths: 'So in everything, do to others what you would have them do to you…' (Matthew 7:12).

The Lord's Prayer

A version of the Lord's prayer is given in Matthew 6:9–13. Rabbis often gave their disciples a form of prayer which contained the main points of their teaching. Jesus highlights three concerns here:

- ❑ God as our Father ('Abba' in Aramaic, Jesus' language. This was a term used by children of their fathers and translates as 'papa' or 'daddy'.)
- ❑ The kingdom of God – God's rule and principles in our lives
- ❑ Forgiveness – we cannot be forgiven unless we forgive.

Fulfilling the Torah

Matthew 5:17–20 concerns the Torah. Jesus says he has not abolished it, but fulfilled it. None of its commandments can be thrown away – a passage that was awkward for the early church as it strove to move away from circumcision and the food laws. Was Jesus just referring to the ethical commandments and not the ritual ones? Perhaps since Jesus lived the perfect life of obedience, something new may be at work for us now. Being sinners, we can never fulfil all of God's laws, but Jesus has done so, and so we can come under his mercy and covering. We can be accepted in and through him.

The Old and the New

Matthew 13:52 says that a teacher of the Law who has come into relationship with Jesus is like a householder who can produce precious treasures, both old and new, from his storeroom. The wisdom of the old Torah can be mixed with the blessings of the gospel for mutual enrichment. Just so, the ancient traditions of some churches today can mix with the fresh winds of Holy Spirit renewal. Not everything has to be 'new' – or 'old' – to be of God, who, after all, is timeless.

Wisdom!

A passage in Matthew 11:25–30 is striking. Some of its language about the Son and the Father is akin to John's Gospel. It contains a portrayal of Jesus as the Wisdom of God incarnate, calling out for people to follow him.

There is also a meaningful call to take his yoke upon our shoulders. Yoking two oxen together was common in the farming of his day; he wants us to walk with him, beside him, and yet to be led by him. He knows us intimately, and will do what is best for us. The yoke is always bespoke – it never chafes!

The Kingdom

The Gospels present a tension between a sense that the kingdom is already here in Jesus and in our hearts, and that it is something yet to come. This is seen in a collection of parables in Matthew 13. The sower, the weeds and the mustard seed parables are about the kingdom growing in our midst, now. The hidden treasure and the pearl parables are about discovering the kingdom right here, now. The net parable is about future judgment and a kingdom coming in all its fullness.

Church

In Matthew 18:15–20, Jesus envisages that there will be some sort of church. 'Church' comes from a Greek word meaning 'gathering' or 'assembly' – it is the people and not the building! He promises that where two or three are gathered in his name, he will be there. Jesus also puts a child right in the centre of his disciples (see Matthew 18:2–4) and urges us to become as children – that is, humble and trusting – to enter the kingdom (see also his invitation to the children in Matthew 19:13–15).

The Two become One?

Matthew sometimes has two items or details when the other Gospels have only one. Jesus heals two blind men in Matthew 20:29–34, whereas Mark 10:46–52 has only one. In Matthew, Jesus enters Jerusalem on a donkey with its colt, whereas the other Gospels have just a single donkey. This is a puzzle. It is good to be honest about some things in scripture that we just do not understand!

Woe!

For a Gospel which has such a Jewish flavour, it is strange to find a catalogue of woes regarding the Pharisees in Matthew 23. The Pharisees were actually a devout bunch on the whole, but they did tend to pile up extra laws and rules based upon human tradition and not the word of God. Jesus attacks those of their number who are not practising what they preach, and pulls the rug from under many of their traditions.

Virgins and Talents

Matthew 25 has these two extra parables, building upon the injunction to watch and to be ready for the coming of the Lord that is found in Mark. The foolish virgins do not bother to get ready for the coming of the bridegroom (one of those exotic Eastern customs lost on a Western readership), and the person who hides his gift misses out on God's blessing. The message is to be ready, and get up and serve! After these parables, the return of Jesus is described as 'the coming of the Son of Man', which harks back to Daniel's vision in Daniel 7:13–14.

Risen!

Matthew adds the story of the Roman rumour that the disciples must have stolen the body, and he has the staggering vision of the risen Jesus that closes his Gospel. Jesus instructs his followers to make disciples of all nations, to baptize in the threefold name of Father, Son and Holy Spirit (though some early Christian communities seem to have baptized in the name of Jesus only), and assures them that he will be with them till the end of time.

KEY VERSES

'All authority in heaven and on earth has been given to me. Therefore go and make disciples of all nations, baptizing them in the name of the Father and of the Son and of the Holy Spirit, and teaching them to obey everything I have commanded you. And surely I am with you always, to the very end of the age.'

Matthew 28:18b–20

JESUS IN MATTHEW

Jesus is the new Moses, fulfilling the old Law and giving a new one. He is Wisdom in the flesh, calling people to take his yoke upon them, and he is the coming Son of Man who has been given all authority (see Daniel 7:14).

QUICK READ

Matthew 1–2 – Birth Stories and Fulfilled Prophecies
Matthew 5–7 – the Sermon on the Mount
Matthew 11:28–30 – the Yoke
Matthew 13 – Parables of the Kingdom
Matthew 18:1–14 – Children and the Church
Matthew 25:1–30 – the Virgins and the Talents
Matthew 28 – the Resurrection

Mark

Mark's Gospel is the shortest one, and is full of rapid action. Jesus is a worker of wonders and full of authority. Three of its sixteen chapters are taken up with the passion and resurrection stories.

Structure

Mark follows the outline presented by Peter in Acts 10:37–43, whereby Jesus begins his ministry after his baptism in the River Jordan at the hands of John the Baptist. He then works in Galilee until his final journey to Jerusalem for the Passover. There he is arrested and put to death, though God raises him to life and the tomb is found to be empty. Around and into this he places collections of sayings of Jesus and healing stories. Large sections of chapters 1 and 2 are concerned with healings, one after another.

Keep It a Secret!

Another key theme that Mark introduces, and which is followed by Luke and Matthew, is the messianic secret. By this, scholars mean that Jesus asks people to keep quiet about who they think he is. He heals someone and asks them not to spread it around (though, naturally, they do!). The demons reveal who he is and he orders them to be quiet. It is only at his trial before the high priest that he publicly owns the titles that he is given. When asked if he is 'the Christ, the Son of the Blessed One,' he replies, 'I am... and you will see the Son of Man sitting at the right hand of the Mighty One and coming on the clouds of heaven' (see Mark 14:61b–62). The request for secrecy is there to preserve Jesus from undue attention from the authorities and from the erroneous expectations of the people.

Messiah/Christ?

'Christ' was the Greek term for the Hebrew word 'messiah'. Both mean 'anointed one', the king, one specially blessed and chosen to lead the people. (Remember that Jewish kings were anointed with holy oil, the oil being a symbol of the Spirit.) The Old Testament looked forward to the coming of the messiah as a great liberator figure. Many expected him to be a mighty (perhaps even a supernatural) warrior, but there are enigmatic passages in the Old Testament that run counter to this. The Servant would be gentle, said Isaiah 42:1–3, and he would suffer for the sins of the people, said Isaiah 53. The Shepherd would be struck and the sheep would be scattered, said Zechariah 13:7.

Jesus refers to these verses in relation to himself (see Mark 8:31–38) and warns his disciples that he is going to die. He also points to the passage in Daniel 7:13–14 about the Son of Man coming on the clouds of heaven. His suffering had to come before this, and Christianity introduced the idea of a twofold coming of the messiah, once in humility and service, and once in power and glory.

The Baptist

John the Baptist features in all four Gospels as a forerunner of Jesus – a prophet called to prepare the people for his coming. The water baptism was a striking symbol of repentance because this was administered to Gentile converts to Judaism. They washed away their unbelief and their idol worship and made a decisive break with the past. To ask people who were born Jews to do this was shocking and scandalous. John dresses like the prophet Elijah and identifies himself with him, quoting from Malachi 3:1. The Jews believed that Elijah would return (somehow) before the coming of the messiah.

Christian baptism came from Jesus and the apostles; this had a different meaning. It was about being forgiven and 'dying and rising' with Christ – i.e. going underwater and coming up again.

The Baptism

Jesus identifies with the Baptist's call for repentance and cleansing, though he has no need to repent as he is God and man. He acts here as a representative Israelite. This marks a transition and the call to begin his ministry. Note the Trinitarian pattern to the call and experience – the Father's voice, the descent of the Spirit and the presence of the Son. Though the term 'Trinity' is not used in the Bible, it is there in essence.

Conflicts

Jesus goes against the ritualism of much of the Judaism of his time, with its oral traditions and taboos. He allows his disciples to pick corn on the sabbath as they are hungry, arguing that the sabbath is made for people to rest and relax and not to be burdened by (see Mark 2:23–28). Jesus rejects the idea that the food laws are essential to holiness, reminding people that what is in the heart is more important than what goes into the stomach (see Mark 7:1–23). He accuses some of making God's word ineffectual because of all their own traditions that have become encrusted over it.

Healings and Miracles

Mark's Gospel is full of healing stories, and Jesus was seen as a healer as well as a teacher from the earliest times. The apostles' preaching (see Acts 2:22) on the day of Pentecost acknowledged this. Even the most ardent sceptics admit that he had some ability to heal, however they explain this. There are fewer miracle stories whereby Jesus exercises a remarkable power over nature, though, such as feeding 5,000 with a few loaves and fish, calming the storm, walking on water or cursing a fig tree. Some cast doubt on these as far-fetched, preferring to read symbolic meanings into them only, and they often can have such inner meanings, such as the calming of the storm suggesting that Jesus brings peace into the storms of our own lives. Some try to give more natural explanations, such as the feeding of the multitude being done by shaming people to share what little food they had with them, and then there was enough. However, we cannot reject the miracles out of hand, for if Jesus was God incarnate, then he was Lord of nature and could operate powers that we do not begin to understand. We need to keep an open mind!

The End

Mark 13 presents a series of predictions about the End and the coming of the Son of Man. Some of the language is highly poetic and symbolic. There is also mention made of the fall of Jerusalem (this happened at the hands of the Romans in AD 70). These two events are telescoped together. Clearly, the early church believed that the End had to come very soon after Jerusalem's fall, though we now realize that there is a much greater delay.

Last Supper

Mark 14:12–26 has one of the earliest accounts of the Last Supper, which was probably a Passover meal. Interestingly, Luke mentions a first cup of wine before Jesus took bread and wine from the table – there are several cups drunk at the Passover. The Last Supper was the start of the eucharist or holy communion, carried on when Christians gather to this day.

Risen

Mark's account of the resurrection is rather truncated. The earliest manuscripts end at Mark 16:8 as the women race away, stunned and afraid, from the empty tomb and its angel, who proclaims Christ's resurrection. The rest of the chapter is a later addition that simply sums up what the other Gospels tell us happened. Was Mark's original ending lost? Was he ending on a dramatic note, knowing that his readers knew the rest of the story anyway? We do not know, but what is important is that the earliest Gospel had a resurrection, and this is consonant with the earliest apostolic preaching as seen in Acts. Without the resurrection there would be no gospel, no 'good news'.

KEY VERSE

'For even the Son of Man did not come to be served, but to serve, and to give his life as a ransom for many.'

Mark 10:45

JESUS IN MARK

Jesus is the Son of God and a wonder worker. This portrait would have appealed to the Romans, who had many stories of gods or outstanding people appearing and working miracles. However, none would ever have allowed themselves to be crucified. The humility and servant nature of Jesus, and his role as a redeemer, was unique.

QUICK READ

Mark 1 – Baptism by John and the Call of the First Disciples

Mark 2 – Healings and Conflict over the Sabbath

Mark 4:35–41 – Calming the Storm

Mark 6:30–44 – Feeding the 5,000

Mark 6:45–52 – Walking on Water
Mark 13 – End times
Mark 16:1–8 – the Resurrection

Luke

Luke's Gospel is written more for a Gentile audience and is a careful account of events. Jesus is the servant and the saviour of all.

Angels and Bethlehem

Luke 1–2 opens the story with birth stories of John the Baptist and Jesus. John is here revealed to be Jesus' cousin. Luke continues with the visit of the angel Gabriel to Mary. Her response to the message that she has been chosen and blessed to bear the Christ child is to humbly submit, saying, 'I am the Lord's servant… May it be to me as you have said' (Luke 1:38). There is a touching scene as Mary goes to stay with her cousin Elizabeth and the baby John leaps for joy in her womb as the Christ child comes into his presence. Two songs follow, one by Mary and one by Zechariah, John's father. Known as the Magnificat and the Benedictus, these are often used in Christian worship today. They celebrate the saving acts of God, and show how he hears the humble.

Luke has the story of the shepherds at Bethlehem, but he does not mention the Magi. The message of the singing angels is good news for all nations, not just for Israel. Though Luke has some different details from Matthew, they both agree that Jesus was born of a virgin and at Bethlehem.

Presentation and Childhood

The infant Jesus is presented in the Temple to be dedicated to God. A 'righteous' and 'devout' man, Simeon, prophesies over him, recognizing God's presence with the child, as does Anna, a widow. Luke adds a later story from when Jesus is 12. Jesus slips away in the hurly-burly of a Passover pilgrimage when the city is crowded, and is found in the Temple, talking with the elders. Jesus is almost old enough for his Bar Mitzvah, when a Jewish male is reckoned to be an adult member of the synagogue.

Mission Statement

In Luke 4:14–30 Jesus reads the lesson at the synagogue in Nazareth, using Isaiah 61:1–2, where good news is announced to the poor and needy. This is an excellent summary of Jesus' mission statement!

Disciples

There are various accounts of the calls of some of the disciples in the Gospels. Luke 5:1–11 has Simon Peter using his boat for Jesus to preach from. Jesus tells him to let down his net and he catches a huge amount of fish. Simon falls to his knees and recognizes the holiness of Jesus. This is similar to the miraculous catch recorded in John 21, though that was much later. Other Gospels simply have Jesus telling Simon Peter to follow him and leave his fishing.

The Plain

Luke reproduces some of the Sermon on the Mount (see Luke 6:17–49), but he has Jesus standing on a level place, a plain. This could have been a level part of the mountain that Matthew mentions. Luke stresses the plain, though, and some think this is symbolic of his desire to say that the gospel is for the Gentiles, too. All are on the same level, gathered together.

The Whore

In Luke 7:36–50 Jesus has his feet washed by a repentant prostitute's tears at a respectable dinner party held by a prominent Pharisee. He accepts and blesses her, using this as a way of teaching about forgiveness. The socially marginalized are drawn to Jesus as a moth is drawn to a flame.

Who is My Neighbour?

One of the parables peculiar to Luke is that of the Good Samaritan (see Luke 10:25–37). Jesus makes a Samaritan the hero. Samaritans were a race who were not accepted as fully Jewish, being descended from tribes settled in the holy land by the Assyrians many years before Jesus' time. They were the butt of much racist abuse. Jesus points out that the ethical demands of the Torah extend beyond race to all people – any human being is our neighbour.

Another famous parable peculiar to Luke is that of the Lost Son (see Luke 15:11–32), usually referred to as the Prodigal Son parable. This teaches about forgiveness and gratitude. The father in this story is like the Lord.

The Little Man

Luke 19:1–10 tells the story of the diminutive tax collector, Zacchaeus. Tax collectors were hated because they worked for the Romans and often cheated the taxpayers. Jesus invites himself to this man's house and declares him forgiven. Zacchaeus responds with great generosity, giving back much money to his community.

Resurrection

Luke adds the story of the road to Emmaus (Luke 24:13–35), when the risen Jesus appears to two disciples. He instructs them about the Old Testament Scriptures and how they pointed to him. Luke has Jesus appearing and disappearing at will, but he is also more solid in his account; he even eats a piece of broiled fish with the disciples.

Yet Jesus is truly beyond flesh and blood at this point. He is transcendent, and he is taken up to heaven at the end of the Gospel. This is the equivalent of Matthew's rousing climax at the end of his Gospel with the great commission. The book of Acts continues the story and adds more detail to the story of Jesus' ascension.

KEY VERSE

'For this son of mine was dead and is alive again; he was lost and is found.'

Luke 15:24

JESUS IN LUKE

Jesus is the servant and the Son of Man who wishes to embrace all nations. He is the redeemer of the world.

QUICK READ

Luke 1–2 – Birth Stories
Luke 4:14–30 – Sermon at Nazareth
Luke 6:17–49 – Sermon on the Plain
Luke 7:36–50 – the Repentant Prostitute
Luke 10:25–37 – the Parable of the Good Samaritan
Luke 15:11–32 – the Parable of the Lost Son
Luke 19:1–10 – Zacchaeus
Luke 24 – the Resurrection Stories

John

John's Gospel is an independent account from the other three. It is a deeply spiritual and theological work wherein Jesus often speaks in long discourses, whereas he uses short sayings and parables in the other Gospels.

The Word

John does not have a birth story, but he starts even earlier, in eternity. The Word was part of God and has always existed. In Hebrew thought, the Word was God's power and creative agent who interacted with the material creation. He was the part of God that is active among us and within us. Jesus is revealed as the Word made flesh (see John 1:14) who dwelt among us. The Greek says that he 'tabernacled' or 'made his tent' with us; this is a reference to the Temple, the place of God's special dwelling upon earth. Jesus was the new Temple; the old had been replaced by a living being. Interestingly, Jesus predicts that the Temple (i.e. his body) will be destroyed, but that he will rebuild it in three days (see John 2:19–22).

The Seven Signs

John uses a special word for the miracles he relates, which is the Greek for 'sign'. The miracles were not just works of wonder, but had a deeply symbolic significance. Scholars discern seven signs

– seven being the perfect number for the Jews:

1. Turning water into wine
2. Healing of the official's son
3. Healing of the man by the pool
4. Feeding the 5,000
5. Jesus walking on water
6. Healing of the blind man
7. The raising of Lazarus from the dead

Only three of these are in the other Gospels (the official's son, the 5,000 and walking on water), though there are examples of the blind seeing and the dead being raised. Interestingly, archaeologists have discovered the remains of the five colonnades mentioned in chapter 5 as being near the city gate. Many see the reference to five as symbolic of the Torah, but there was an actual place like this, too.

The changing of water into wine can be read symbolically as the coming of the new covenant after the old. The wine of the gospel is an improvement upon the water of the Torah.

The Cleansing of the Temple

Some of John's chronology is different from that of the other Gospels. He has several visits to Jerusalem rather than one main one at the end of Jesus' life. He places the cleansing of the Temple at the start of Jesus' ministry rather than at the end. (The money changers were in the outer precincts of the Temple, where they changed foreign money into shekels, for only Jewish coins were allowed within the inner precincts. They charged high interest on the exchanges.) Perhaps John has placed this deliberately, as it was symbolic of Jesus' cleansing and refining ministry towards Judaism as a whole. The Evangelists felt free to move some sayings and incidents around to make a point.

Living Water

Jesus speaks to a Samaritan woman about living water, which is the bubbling up of the Holy Spirit that Jesus offers to all who believe (see John 4:13–14). He sees the arguments between Jews and Samaritans over which mountain is holy – Zion or Gerazim – as being utterly irrelevant. 'God is spirit,' he says, 'and his worshippers must worship in spirit and in truth' (John 4:24). It's the reality of our faith, of what we are inside that counts.

Bread of Life

John uses the account of the feeding of the 5,000 to launch into one of his long Jesus discourses. Jesus declares himself to be 'the bread of life', just as he declares himself to be the giver of living water. He furthers this imagery with his striking command in John 6:53–57 about eating and drinking him into our lives.

More Water...

In John 7:37–39 Jesus speaks of the streams of living water that will flow from within the believer. The Jews hoped that a miraculous river would flow from the Temple as Ezekiel had described (see Ezekiel 47). Jesus is that river, and the Spirit will flow out of each believer who receives him. Jesus speaks of the Spirit more fully in John chapters 14–16 as the Helper or the Comforter, terms that describe one who comes alongside to help when he has gone.

I Am...

Jesus' long discourses in John often have seeds of thought behind them that can parallel Jesus' one-liners in the other Gospels. Thus, his speech to Nicodemus about being born again (John 3) is akin to statements about becoming as a child in Matthew 18:1–4. John takes things much further, and has Jesus saying 'I am...' several times, such as in his statements about being 'the bread of life' or 'the light of the world'. The 'I am' reflects the Hebrew name for the Lord, Yahweh, which means 'I am who I am' (see Exodus 3:14).

No Last Supper?

John 13 has the disciples in the upper room where the Last Supper took place, but there is no account of sharing the bread and wine in John. Instead, Jesus washes the disciples' feet there. Perhaps John, with his use of bread and wine in a number of stories and sayings, wants us to go deeper, hinting that holy communion is important at various points in the gospel – water into wine; bread of life; the true vine. John makes us work much more than the other Gospel writers. (Note, also, the frequent use of water as a symbol, possibly being an indirect reference to baptism.)

The Vine

John has his own image of Jesus and the church – we are branches and Jesus is the vine. John does not teach an inner spiritual enlightenment that is individualistic, instead saying that we are called into fellowship with Jesus and one another. The vine image also shows Jesus fulfilling Old Testament hopes, as Israel is compared with a vine (see Isaiah 5:1–7).

Wounds

John's Jesus has his side pierced with a lance to prove that he is dead (see John 19:31–37). Medical science agrees that the blood and water that flowed would have been the expected physical result of crucifixion.

Risen

The resurrection is numinous but solid for John. Jesus appears to Mary Magdalene in the garden by the tomb. He is not shining with light, and she thinks that he is the gardener until he speaks to her. He appears, disappears and passes through locked doors, but he invites doubting Thomas to place his fingers in his wounds (see John 20:24–29). Thomas's confession, 'My Lord and my God!' declares Jesus to be unambiguously divine.

Jesus in this whole Gospel has a more supernatural aura about him, though he is a real flesh and blood figure. Some wonder if John's account is coloured by the events of the resurrection, whereas the other writers are a little more down-to-earth about the humanity of Jesus, with shafts of glory shining through. Some wonder if the long discourses were inspired by the risen Lord rather than said during his life on earth. Some see these as expansions of short sayings in the other Gospels (e.g. the passage in John 3 about being 'born again' develops the idea in Matthew 19:14 about 'becoming like children'). Of course, it may have been that he simply taught the disciples privately in more depth.

John finishes with the miraculous catch of fish (see John 21) as he calls Peter and the others back after they had fled Jerusalem. The catch would have reminded Peter of his initial call (see Luke 5:1–11), and the charcoal fire would have brought to mind that cold courtyard where Peter denied having known Jesus. Jesus let Peter see and know that he knew him inside out, and he still offered forgiveness.

An Additional Story

There is a marvellous piece of floating tradition that early manuscripts of John do not include. We do not know where it came from, but it smacks of an authentic memory of Jesus, through and through! This is John 7:53 – 8:11 and the story of the woman taken in adultery. Jesus does not condemn her, but invites anyone without sin to cast the first stone. It was a clever way of subverting the harsh commands of the Torah without directly breaking them.

KEY VERSE

'For God so loved the world that he gave his one and only Son, that whoever believes in him shall not perish but have eternal life.'

John 3:16

JESUS IN JOHN

Jesus is the eternal Word of God made flesh, the new Temple in person, and the one who can speak with divine authority as 'I am…' Yet this God-man really was flesh and blood and really died on the cross.

QUICK READ

John 1:1–14 – The Word
John 2:1–11 – Water into Wine
John 3:1–21 – Nicodemus and Being Born Again
John 4:1–42 – the Woman at the Well
John 6:25–59 – the Bread of Life
John 14–16 – the Helper and the True Vine
John 20–21 – the Resurrection Stories

The Acts of the Apostles

The Acts is the second volume of Luke's work, continuing the story after Jesus' ascension and telling how the first church developed.

Glimpses of History

Acts does not fill in all the gaps as it jumps about from Jerusalem and the holy land to Ethiopia and the missionary journeys of Paul. Much of the book is taken up with this latter material, and the various references to 'we' in this part of the narrative suggest that Luke was a travelling companion of Paul, or, at the very least, that he had access to travel diaries. Historians and archaeologists marvel at the amount of incidental details that are scattered throughout the book, such as the names of minor officials (e.g. Gallio in Corinth, mentioned in Acts 18) for whose existence evidence exists in the form of inscriptions.

Acts does leave us, however, with many unanswered questions about the early church, not the least of which is Paul's fate. The book closes with him under house arrest, waiting to appeal to the emperor. (Christian tradition says that he was martyred.)

Going Up!

Acts opens with the ascension of Jesus – his return to heaven

 40 days after his resurrection. Acts 1:9 does not actually say that he continues to float up and up and away into the sky. He begins to rise – a symbol of exaltation and lordship – and then a cloud envelops him. The cloud, in the Bible, is a symbol for the Holy Spirit and the glory of God, the *shekinah*, in Hebrew. (Note that this cloud was also there at the transfiguration in Matthew 17:5, and when Solomon dedicated the Temple in 1 Kings 8:10–11.) Jesus is translated into the dimension of heaven; we do not have to believe that it is up above the sky somewhere.

Come, Holy Spirit...

Jesus tells his disciples to wait for the coming of the Holy Spirit. They are only just rebuilding their shattered faith, and they do not go out on their missions until God's power comes upon them. This is a key to understanding both the book of Acts and the rise of the early church. The church is not a human movement in essence, but divine, no matter how much its members mess things up along the way. The Spirit moves people to repentance, brings rebirth, opens doors, guides people to the right places, and touches their words with an anointing of power and grace.

The Spirit comes in power on the Day of Pentecost, a Jewish celebration of the giving of the Torah that was 50 days after Easter. The disciples have a visionary experience of rushing wind and fire – two vivid symbols of the Spirit's power and holiness. They begin to speak in tongues spontaneously, and many pilgrims hear their own languages. 'Tongues', *glossolalia* in the Greek, is a special prayer and praise language that some people receive when they open themselves to the Spirit. Some people seem to speak actual languages, some might speak those of angels (see 1 Corinthians 13 and 14) and some might speak a personal prayer language that has rhythm and grammar but is unknown and idiosyncratic. More on this in the material on 1 Corinthians.

The Apostolic Preaching

Various passages in Acts reveal glimpses of sermons by the apostles, including how they read Old Testament Scriptures in the light of Jesus. They give us a framework of early belief and doctrine which was developed and refined as time went by. Acts 2:22–24 has a raw, primitive feel, with Jesus presented as 'a man accredited by God' who was raised up and has become Lord and Christ. The implications of why this man should have been so would have been worked out later, in the doctrine of the incarnation. Hence we can see that the author is drawing upon early and accurate material here.

Acts 8:26–39 tells the story of the apostle Philip and the Ethiopian eunuch. This uses the text of Isaiah 53 to preach Jesus. This passage was a key proof text for the early Christians.

Tensions

Was the first church perfect, pure and holy? Not quite, simply because it was made up of sinful human beings. There were various tensions. Early on, we see problems in Acts 6 between the Hellenists – Greek-speaking Jewish Christians – and the Hebrew-speaking ones. The apostles have to ordain a group of deacons (servants) to oversee the needs of the former. Paul and Barnabas fall out and cannot work together (Acts 15:36–40). The Jewish believers do not know what to do with Gentile converts at first – should they become Jews as well as Christians? These issues go deep and underlie many of Paul's letters. Gradually, it is agreed that Gentile converts do not need to be circumcised or to keep all the ritual laws of the Torah (see Acts 15:1–29).

Persecution

The apostles do not always have it easy. Stephen the deacon is stoned to death, Peter is imprisoned, and James, brother of John, is killed. Paul (formerly Saul) had been an enemy of the church until his conversion on the road to Damascus (see Acts 9). This is testimony to the grace and power of God to turn bitterness into joy and an enemy into a brother. Note how the risen Jesus says that he is being persecuted and not just his followers – is this the root of Paul's later exposition of the church as the Body of Christ (1 Corinthians 12)? Paul himself undergoes various trials, beatings, imprisonments and even a shipwreck (see Acts 27:39–44). However, there is grace and power – sometimes eyes are blinded, prison doors opened and mobs are dismissed. Sometimes people have to bear suffering and even martyrdom. We deal with mysteries here.

To the Gentiles

Paul is set apart with Barnabas to go out on a mission (Acts 13:1–4) and three missionary journeys follow around Asia Minor, Greece and into Italy. Paul follows the trade routes and goes to the synagogues first, as the message is to the Jew first and then to the Gentile. Groups of Gentile 'Godfearers' gather outside the synagogues, worshipping one God but not prepared to become Jews. They listen to Paul and respond, while the Jews do not always prove so receptive. Gradually, Paul finds himself an apostle to the Gentiles, teaching them and establishing churches.

Paul's final visit to Jerusalem nearly causes a riot, and shows that tensions still exist between Jewish and Gentile believers, as zealots condemn him for forsaking the Torah (see Acts 21:27 – 22:29).

Fluid Structure

This rapid growth of a new religious movement does not proceed with a clear rule book in hand, as we can see from the Jewish/Gentile tensions alone. The Spirit often comes when people are baptized and have hands laid upon them, but not always. With the Roman Cornelius, the Spirit comes while Peter is speaking, before Cornelius is baptized (Acts 10:44–48). Others have had some form of baptism but have heard nothing about a Holy Spirit, and the apostles' hands do the trick (see Acts 19:1–7). Let us remember that even though churches today have their own norms for how to initiate people, God is sovereign and the Spirit blows where he wills.

KEY VERSE

'But you will receive power when the Holy Spirit comes on you; and you will be my witnesses in Jerusalem, and in all Judea and Samaria, and to the ends of the earth.'

Acts 1:8

JESUS IN ACTS

In the early preaching, Jesus is Lord and messiah – so appointed by the resurrection – as well as the Holy and Righteous One. He is also the Suffering Servant of Isaiah 53 and the Lord of his body on earth, which is the church made up of his followers. He is the one who will turn people from the power of Satan to God (see Acts 26:18) and who still heals and delivers through his followers.

QUICK READ

Acts 1:1–11 – Ascension and Promise of the Holy Spirit

Acts 2 – Pentecost and the Early Preaching

Acts 6–7 – Stephen's Message and Martyrdom

Acts 9 – Saul's Conversion

Acts 15 – Tensions between Jewish and Gentile Christians

Acts 16 – Paul's Adventures in Philippi

Acts 28:11–31 – Paul in Rome

Introduction to the Letters

Most of the books of the New Testament are letters written by various apostles – mostly by Paul, in fact. It might seem strange to have this collection in Holy Writ, but they were written to challenge, encourage or teach various churches which were often the converts of the apostle concerned. They contain absolute gems of doctrine and insight which still speak today, although the social and historical circumstances are different.

There are scholars who think that disciples of the apostles wrote some of them, authoring them anonymously and naming them after their teachers out of respect. This could have been a first-century custom, but others follow the traditional teaching that they were written by who they say they were. (Even the most liberal, radical scholars believe that Paul definitely wrote Romans, 1 and 2 Corinthians and Galatians himself.) Whoever actually did the writing, though, spiritual truth is spiritual truth.

They were usually written on the hoof, as the apostle travelled about or sat in prison. They are generally heartfelt outpourings, as opposed to detailed, careful expositions or treatises of systematic theology. They do contain theology and strongly argued ideas, but they are personal mailings, revealing much about the heart of the writer and various incidental details. They thus show how experiential the gospel was to the apostles; it burned in their souls and was not just head knowledge.

They do not give us a tidy scheme of things, but bits and pieces, and we suspect at times that we are overhearing parts of teaching that also had carried on orally (such as material about the Lord's return) and which is largely lost to us. There is enough – more than enough – though, to feed us, guide us and build the doctrine of Christ.

Romans

The Letter to the Romans is the deepest exposition of Paul's theology of grace and justification by faith. This letter is closer to being a theological treatise than any other.

Wrath and Failure

The opening sections of Romans are not lighthearted reading. Paul trawls through the sinfulness of humanity, starting with the pagans and then going on to the Jews. Both pagans and Jews have light from God to guide them – the Gentiles have the light of conscience (see Romans 2:14–15) and the Jews have the Torah or law of Moses. Paul mentions the lustfulness of much of pagan life in the Roman empire, linking idol worship and sexual immorality. He castigates men and women who have unnatural desires for same-sex relationships. Some modern religious scholars feel that Paul's focus here was on people who had freely chosen this path by becoming involved in pagan temple prostitution. Members of today's homosexual community who claim an innate orientation are seen by many scholars as not being in the same category. What causes such an orientation is not known. This is obviously a source of much debate currently, though both sides agree that such an orientation is not sinful in and of itself. Nonetheless, acting on it is seen to be so by orthodox Christianity.

The Law

Paul indicates, using himself as an example, that the Jews who have the Torah do not always follow it. The Torah is righteous in itself, but it has no power to make people righteous. It is an external moral code, he says, that is powerless to change hearts. Paul appeals to a new and living way to serve God. Through faith in Jesus and his death, we can be accepted and come into God's presence, even though we are still sinners (see Romans 3:21–31). Paul spends much time explaining this.

Abraham

Paul turns to the story of Father Abraham, the great ancestor of the Jews (see Romans 4:1–25). He was accepted by God ('justified') because of his faith, says Paul, who refers to Genesis 15:6 when he says, 'Abraham believed God, and it was credited to him as righteousness.' This was not an abstract, intellectual faith. Abraham had to prove his faith by getting up and moving; good works followed from his act of trust.

Abraham trusted and was accepted before the coming of the Law. He received a promise that his seed would spread and inherit the nations, a promise that had nothing to do with the Law. Paul sees Jesus as the fulfilment of that promise, the seed of Abraham. We enter into a justified, accepted relationship with God through Jesus, apart from the Law. Elsewhere, Paul argues that the Law was a sort of schoolmaster or supervisor, preparing God's 'pupils' for Christ (see Galatians 3:24). Moses and the

Torah were an interim arrangement, a shadow of things to come, even though they taught much that was good and brought many blessings.

Death and Life

Paul contrasts Adam with Jesus in Romans 5:12–21. Death came through the disobedience of the first man, but life came through the second Adam, and we die to our old life and rise to new life through baptism and the inner grace of the Holy Spirit. In Romans 6:1–14, Paul speaks of baptism as an entry into the death of Christ – i.e. into all its atoning, cleansing power. Paul even uses secular law as an example, showing how a married woman is bound to her husband only while he lives. She is free when he dies, and in the same way a believer who has 'died and risen' with Christ is free from the demands of the Torah. Going down under the water and coming up is a symbol of dying and rising with Christ. (Note that Paul is concerned with the inner meaning of baptism and not how the ceremony is undertaken, whether by sprinkling or total immersion.)

Struggles and Spiritual Power

Paul admits that even with grace, baptism and spiritual regeneration, we struggle with our natural, fleshly selves. We have something new – the Spirit – in something old: our selves. It is like power steering in a car. If it is turned off, we struggle, but when it is on, we glide. In Romans 8, Paul speaks of the new and higher law of the Spirit at work in us. If we listen, obey and are in tune with this, then the 'power steering' is on and there is life, health and peace within. Through the Spirit we can address God as 'Abba' just as Jesus did and we are no longer servants or slaves but sons (Romans 8:15–16). In Roman times the sons inherited the father's assets; the servants did not.

Paul goes deeper still and says profound things about the groanings and struggles of the Spirit in creation as it seeks to renew a fallen world (Romans 8:18–27). The Spirit even prays for us and within us, and many Christians are aware of this happening in their spirits during deep prayer.

The Jews

Paul's teaching caused trouble with some Jewish Christians who still kept the Torah, and did so with joy and with gratitude for their inheritance as Jews. Paul seems to have struggled with the Law as a Jew, feeling compelled and condemned. Zealots who are quick to condemn others are usually masking their own self-hatred. This does not weaken his arguments, though, for they are the very essence of the gospel of grace. There is nothing wrong with choosing to keep the Torah rituals, Paul says, as long as these are not imposed upon Gentile converts, for that would make the rituals as essential as Jesus for salvation. (Today some Messianic Jews choose to keep the Torah out of deference to their Jewishness, but admit that they do not have to.)

Paul is careful to praise the Jews – his own race, after all – and to see them as still close to God's heart. He reminds Gentile converts that they are a branch that has been grafted onto an older tree (Israel), and they should be eternally grateful to his people for the prophets and the gifts of God (see Romans 11:11–32), though he grieves over the Jews' hardness of heart.

KEY VERSES

'Therefore, since we have been justified through faith, we have peace with God through our Lord Jesus Christ, through whom we have gained access by faith into this grace in which we now stand.'

Romans 5:1–2

JESUS IN ROMANS

Jesus is the Promised Seed of Abraham who will bring blessing to the nations. He has freed us from the demands of the Law by his death, and we can enter a relationship with God through a living faith in him.

QUICK READ

Romans 1:18 – 2:29 – God's Wrath and Human Sin

Romans 4 – Abraham and the Promise

Romans 5:12–21 – Adam and Jesus

Romans 6:1–14 – the Death of Jesus and Baptism

Romans 8 – the Spirit's Power and Life

Romans 9–11 – Israel

1 and 2 Corinthians

Paul's letters to the Corinthians cover many ethical and practical problems, but they also reveal deep spiritual insights along the way.

1 Corinthians and Problems

Corinth was a cosmopolitan city full of trade, travellers and pagan temples. The church there had particular problems and reading about this should disabuse us of the idea that all churches in apostolic times were pristine and pure! Paul mentions a string of negatives:

❑ Disunity (1 Corinthians 1:10–17; 3) – Factions have developed based upon personalities and their teaching.

❑ Immorality (1 Corinthians 5) – A man is having sex with his stepmother. Paul declares that this is unacceptable (even for pagans!) and if he does not repent, he is to be expelled from the church.

❑ Lawsuits (1 Corinthians 6:1–11) – Brothers are taking each other to court rather than settling their differences between themselves. This makes a mockery of Christ and Paul asks them to forgive and to even bear the insult and wrong if necessary.

❑ Idols and food (1 Corinthians 8) – Some believers are upset that others eat in the temple markets where the meat has been offered to pagan gods. Paul says that this does not matter in itself – for the gods are not real gods, after all – saying, 'we are no worse if we do not eat, and no better if we do' (8:8). He appeals to them to respect the weaker faith of some of their brethren, though, and to abstain if this causes them offence. A contemporary example might be the use of alcohol.

❑ Taking communion unworthily (1 Corinthians 11:17–34) – The early Christians took the bread and wine in the context of a meal, an *agape* ('love feast'). Some in Corinth are not sharing food and are ignoring others. This makes a mockery of communion. Paul reveals a strong sense of Christ's presence and blessing through taking communion and he repeats the words of Jesus from the Last Supper, using them as liturgy.

❑ Spiritual gifts (1 Corinthians 12–14) – The Spirit brings special gifts, as glimpsed in the Acts of the Apostles. These are listed in 1 Corinthians 12:4–11 and they are supernatural. There are healings, words of prophecy and special insight into situations ('knowledge'), as well as speaking in tongues, for example. Speaking in tongues in particular seems to have caused a frenzy at Corinth, with people all gabbling away at the same time in a spirit of competition. Paul reminds them in 14:32 that this is the least of the gifts and should be under the control of the speaker. He says that such utterances should be respectful and peaceful, with one speaking at a time and another seeking to interpret.

The gifts of the Spirit are supernatural but not paranormal. Things such as clairvoyance and ESP, if they really are abilities that some have, are not from the Spirit. Spiritual gifts glorify Jesus as Lord (see 1 Corinthians 12:3–6) and come from his power alone.

❑ False doctrine (1 Corinthians 15) – Some are teaching that Jesus had not been physically raised. This might have been an early form of a later heresy known as Gnosticism. Gnostics flourished in the 2nd century AD and taught that Jesus' body did not rise, for they saw matter as inferior to spirit. The 'resurrection', they felt, was really an inner, personal rising as a form of spiritual enlightenment (the concept is almost Buddhist, in fact!). Paul gives a long exposition and defence of resurrection, explaining that the resurrection body is not bound by matter.

Wisdom and Love

In the midst of all the disputes, Paul writes moving words about the wisdom of God and the nature of love. In 1 Corinthians 1:18 through chapter 2, he speaks about the wisdom and power revealed in Christ through the cross. It is not in fine words and rhetoric that the Spirit moves, but in obedient hearts, from humility and weakness. In chapter 13 he writes the famous hymn to love which is heard at many a marriage. This is to urge the believers to respect each other and not to worship in a spirit of factionalism and competition.

Odd Bits

Paul argues that women should keep silent in church and cover their heads (see 1 Corinthians 11:1–16; 14:34–35). This seems restrictive and against his views that the Spirit comes upon all and brings freedom, but unveiled women could be seen as prostitutes then and some of the believing women were unruly at Corinth. These instructions are generally regarded as no longer relevant. Paul also argues that being single is better than being married (see 1 Corinthians 7:8–9). He seems to think that this is because the Lord will soon return and there is much to be done. He was wrong about this, and though there is a gift of celibacy, marriage is also a blessing.

2 Corinthians and Resolutions

In 2 Corinthians, Paul urges the Corinthians to be reconciled. If the brother who has slept with his stepmother has repented, he should be forgiven and accepted back. Paul writes of the 'yes' of God in Christ, and the law of grace that the Spirit brings. There is a real liberty when the Spirit is present (see 2 Corinthians

3:17), but not libertinism. What is immoral is immoral. Paul has been given the ministry of reconciliation that follows from God's great reconciling act in Christ.

One problem seems to have occurred over marriage to unbelievers. Paul urges believers to marry believers, and not to be joined together with a spiritual opposite, which he calls being 'unequally yoked' (2 Corinthians 6:14–16). However, in 1 Corinthians 7:12–16, he does caution that converts to the faith should not leave unbelieving spouses for that reason.

Collections

A famine has arisen in Judea and Paul is organizing collections from his churches for the saints in Jerusalem. He appeals to the Corinthians to be generous and preaches Christ in the process, saying, 'For you know the grace of our Lord Jesus Christ, that though he was rich, yet for your sakes he became poor, so that you through his poverty might become rich' (2 Corinthians 8:9). Paul adds the most direct advice on giving found in the New Testament, which is an appeal to the heart rather than a specific amount: 'Each man should give what he has decided in his heart to give, not reluctantly or under compulsion, for God loves a cheerful giver' (2 Corinthians 9:7).

Conflicts

Conflicts over authority still seem to be around. There are those whom Paul calls 'false apostles' who are trying to undermine his teaching (see 2 Corinthians 11). This seems to stem from his views about circumcision and the Law.

Visionary

Paul describes a transcendent experience in 2 Corinthians 12:2–4. By the 'third heaven' he means the abode of God and the angels, rather than that of demons (second heaven) or the earth and sky (first heaven). He cannot describe this, for it was ineffable – a mark of a genuine encounter with God!

KEY VERSES

1 CORINTHIANS

'And if Christ has not been raised, your faith is futile; you are still in your sins.'

1 Corinthians 15:17

2 CORINTHIANS

'Now the Lord is the Spirit, and where the Spirit of the Lord is, there is freedom.'

2 Corinthians 3:17

JESUS IN CORINTHIANS

Jesus is the wisdom and power of God who is truly risen. He is God's 'yes' to humanity and a spreading spiritual fragrance (2 Corinthians 2:14). He made himself poor that we might be rich.

1 Corinthians 1:18 – 2:16 – the Wisdom of God

1 Corinthians 6:1–11 – Trouble Involving Lawsuits

1 Corinthians 11:17–34 – the Lord's Supper

1 Corinthians 12 – Spiritual Gifts

1 Corinthians 13 – the Hymn to Love

1 Corinthians 15 – the Resurrection

2 Corinthians 3 – Ministers of a New Covenant and the Spirit of Life

2 Corinthians 5:11–21 – God's Reconciliation in Christ

2 Corinthians 9 – Giving

Galatians

The Galatian letter repeats some of the key themes of Romans and teaches grace and justification by faith and not works.

Paul's Authority

In Galatians 1–2, Paul begins by asserting his credentials as an apostle – he is a witness of the risen Christ and he has been accepted by the apostles at Jerusalem. He relates his career and launches into a rebuke of Peter's giving in to the Jews and refusing to eat with Gentile believers. Paul urges his readers to accept no other gospel even if an angel comes to preach it. He does not want to sell them short.

Justification by Faith

Galatians 2:15 – 3:29 presents the case for justification by faith – being accepted by God because of belief in what Jesus has done for us. He repeats his idea that if we die with Christ in baptism then the Law has no hold over us, and that the Spirit comes by grace, not by earning his favour.

He appeals to the story of Abraham, who was counted righteous because of his faith long before the Law came, and who received the promise of a future seed and blessing. Through Jesus, we are all children of God, heirs of the promise and children of Abraham.

Hagar and Sarah

He digs deeper into the Abraham story and compares Jews and Christians with Hagar and Sarah, the concubine and wife of Abraham, respectively (see Galatians 4:21–31). The slave-woman is under the Law, but the wife bears the children of the promise. We are like Isaac – children of the promise.

No Circumcision

Paul urges the Galatians not to listen to the Judaizing Christians who want them to be circumcised. If they do, then Christ is of no use to them – they might as well embrace the whole Torah. These are old covenant externals that are not equal in import with Jesus and the grace of God (see Galatians 5:1–18).

KEY VERSE

'There is neither Jew nor Greek, slave nor free, male nor female, for you are all one in Christ Jesus.'

Galatians 3:28

JESUS IN GALATIANS

Jesus is the one who frees people from the demands of the Law and is the child of promise.

QUICK READ

Galatians 1:6–10 – Accept No Other Gospel
Galatians 3:15–29 – Children of Abraham and the Promise
Galatians 4:21–31 – Hagar and Sarah
Galatians 5:22–26 – the Fruit of the Spirit

Ephesians

The Ephesian letter is a mature spiritual reflection on the mystery of Christ.

Spiritual Blessings

Ephesians 1–2 relate how God has poured out every spiritual blessing upon a believer through Christ. We are sealed by the Spirit – an image of ownership taken from the marketplace, where pots were stamped with a seal to show that they had been bought. Jesus is the fullness of all and is head of the church. The 'fullness' was an important theological term then, denoting the power of the High God and not a lesser deity. Jesus, through his death, has made peace, breaking down walls of hostility and calling Jew and Greek into one new man.

Wisdom

Paul declares in chapter 3 that the wisdom of God was kept hidden for ages and has now been made known in Christ. It is beyond knowledge and words, though it can be felt and known. The use of the term 'mystery' for God's saving acts is significant here, for the Roman world abounded with mystery cults which had secret initiation rites and esoteric knowledge. The gospel is an open secret, an unveiled mystery for all to see.

Ascendance and Gifts

In Ephesians 4, Paul takes an Old Testament scripture (Psalm 68:18) and sees Jesus in it. Jesus ascended on high after coming down to the earth, and he has showered gifts upon the church. He urges people to live in the Spirit and avoid the works of the flesh. Ephesians 5:18–20 encourages people to keep praising and being filled with the Spirit.

Wives and Husbands

Paul's words about men and women in Ephesians 5:22–33 are

beautiful but controversial today. He reveals that the church is Christ's bride, and that men should love their wives as Christ loves the church. He teaches male headship, though, which causes many debates today, with different views in different churches. Was this meant for all time as a part of nature, or was it simply part of the society then? Whatever the case, Paul softens male headship considerably with his instructions on loving and sacrificing for the wife. The abuse of his advice through the ages is an aberration of his teaching.

Slaves and Masters

In Ephesians 6:5–9, Paul accepts that slavery is a part of his society, which is unthinkable for us today. He does, however, preach mutual respect and goodwill between slaves and masters, even giving slaves rights as brothers in Christ. It may be that this helped sow the seeds for the later abolitionists.

Spiritual Warfare

The appeal to put on spiritual armour (i.e. being in right relationship with God and in obedience to him) is because the Christian faces spiritual battles behind the scenes (see Ephesians 6:10–18). There are deeper forces at work than just the personal. His language of 'rulers, authorities' is sometimes seen today as referring to the unseen power of ungodly structures and systems in our lives that have to be dismantled. Others believe that spiritual, demonic forces are behind these systems, too.

KEY VERSES

'For he himself is our peace, who has made the two one and has destroyed the barrier, the dividing wall of hostility, by abolishing in his flesh the law with its commandments and regulations.'

Ephesians 2:14–15

JESUS IN EPHESIANS

Jesus is the fullness of God in bodily form, and the head of the church. He is the heavenly bridegroom about to return for his earthly bride, the church.

QUICK READ

Ephesians 1:3–14 – Spiritual Blessings in Christ

Ephesians 2:14–22 – Reconciliation in Christ

Ephesians 5:22–33 – Wives and Husbands

Ephesians 6:10–18 – Spiritual Warfare

Philippians

Philippians contains majestic teaching about the servanthood of Jesus and how the cross dethrones our confidence in 'the flesh' – our own egos and abilities.

Giving Up

Paul is still struggling with disputes about his authority and the demands of the Torah, and he stresses the power of the Spirit and how we must live by that (see Philippians 1:19–26). He suddenly speaks of the humility of Jesus, and many think he is quoting an early Christian hymn or confession of faith (Philippians 2:6–11). If that is correct, then it would place this section of the text earlier than his letter, which dates to some time in the 50s AD. The piece in question has a strong and full confession of the divinity of Jesus. His is the name above all names, that of Yahweh. The end of it uses Isaiah 45:23, where the Lord's name is proclaimed as the highest.

Faith and the Cross

In chapter 3, Paul reminds his opponents of his pedigree according to the flesh: a Pharisee, a Jew, and one who was zealous for the Law. However, he counts all of that as nothing (the Greek word is very strong, and 'dung' is a polite translation!). He has given his life to Christ and has been crucified with him. He has opened up to the power of the Spirit to change him and renew him.

Needs

Paul closes the letter with an appeal for the believers to trust God and to commit their needs to him, saying that he will answer from his riches (Philippians 4:19). Earlier, he says that peace will be theirs if they bring their petitions before God (Philippians 4:4–7).

KEY VERSES

'… that at the name of Jesus every knee should bow, in heaven and on earth and under the earth, and every tongue confess that Jesus Christ is Lord, to the glory of God the Father.'

Philippians 2:10–11

JESUS IN PHILIPPIANS

Jesus has been exalted high over all, carrying the very name of God.

QUICK READ

Philippians 2:6–11 – the Hymn to Christ

Philippians 3 – No Confidence in the Flesh

Philippians 4:4–19 – Prayer and Needs

Colossians

Paul repeats some of his key themes in this letter, but it has a deeply spiritual and mystical appreciation of Jesus and advice for those who are falling back into fleshly rules and regulations.

The Firstborn

Colossians 1:15–20 might be an early Christian hymn or confession of faith that Paul is quoting. Jesus is 'the firstborn of all creation', meaning its chief and head. This does not mean that he actually had a beginning – he existed from eternity. Just as the firstborn son was heir to the king, Jesus is the Lord of all. Again, he has the fullness of God in him; he is no lesser deity but part of the highest God.

Dead Rules

The Colossians are tending to follow strict rules about seasons, the sabbath and food laws (whether Jewish or pagan – there were vegetarian cults with odd items that were taboo such as beans!) He reminds them that all these things are shadows of the reality that came in Christ. He died to disarm all evil powers and to declare us accepted and forgiven (see Colossians 2:13–15).

Holy Living

Paul gives a summary of instructions for holy living, avoiding immorality, loving the brethren and following the Spirit in Colossians 3.

KEY VERSE

'See to it that no one takes you captive through hollow and deceptive philosophy, which depends on human tradition and the basic principles of this world rather than on Christ.'

Colossians 2:8

JESUS IN COLOSSIANS

The risen Jesus takes on cosmic proportions, being the firstborn of creation and the fullness of God.

QUICK READ

Colossians 1:15–23 – Christ the Firstborn

Colossians 2:9–15 – the Fullness and Power of Christ

Colossians 2:16–23 – Do Not Be Bound by Human Rules

1 and 2 Thessalonians

The Thessalonian letters are gently pastoral, not having to deal with any disputes. They also contain material about the Lord's return.

Longing to See You

Paul writes to the Thessalonians out of a pastor's heart, having helped to birth their church and nurture them in faith. He relates how he felt like a father to them, encouraging them as his own children (1 Thessalonians 2:11–12). They responded to the word and experienced the power of the Spirit (1 Thessalonians 1:4–5). Paul was unable to visit them again and so he sent Timothy, one of his companions, who brought an encouraging report of their growth (1 Thessalonians 3:6–13).

The Lord's Return

The end of 1 Thessalonians chapter 4 and the beginning of chapter 5 deal with the second coming of Jesus. Those who have died will be raised when he returns and will meet him first, followed by those left alive. They will be 'caught up together with them in the clouds' (4:17). The reference to the clouds harks back to Daniel 7:13 and the Son of Man who comes on the clouds. This idea is sometimes known as the rapture, though this term occurs nowhere in the Bible. Some interpret this to mean that Christians will be removed from the earth for a time before the Lord returns in judgment (see also Matthew 24:36–41), though the text seems to imply that everything will happen more or less at once – archangel's trumpet, Lord returns, dead rise, Christians are caught up.

Man of Lawlessness

Second Thessalonians 2:1–12 adds more details about the return, describing an enigmatic 'man of lawlessness' who will rebel against the Lord, perform Satanic signs and wonders and deceive people. The Lord will not return until this happens and then he will destroy the evil figure. There is something about a mysterious agent (The Spirit? An archangel?) holding back this evil man until the right time. His identity might have been common knowledge in the 1st-century church, but we are left in the dark today. Later tradition calls this evil man the 'antichrist' and many early Christians assumed that the Emperor Nero was this man because of his cruelty and persecution of the church.

Certainly this whole concept is an elaboration on the hints found in the Gospels, such as in Mark 13. Paul never teaches on this elsewhere, but it is certain that there was an oral tradition about the Lord's return circulating in the early church. We catch glimpses of it here and there (note Mark's 'let the reader understand' aside in 13:14) and it pops up to the greatest extent in Revelation.

Don't Be Idle

Paul warns the Thessalonians against idleness (2 Thessalonians 3:6–15) and urges them to work for a living as he did when staying with them. (Elsewhere, Paul is said to have had a trade as a tent maker.) It is interesting to know that Paul and the early Christians lived in a religious climate which expected the End to come at any moment. This might have led some to withdraw from society, but Paul says rather that people should carry on as normal, being alert, faithful and responsible, that the Lord may find them doing what they should be doing when he comes back.

KEY VERSES

1 THESSALONIANS

'For we know, brothers loved by God, that he has chosen you, because our gospel came to you not simply with words, but also with power, with the Holy Spirit and with deep conviction.'

1 Thessalonians 1:4–5

'We pray this so that the name of our Lord Jesus may be glorified in you, and you in him, according to the grace of our God and the Lord Jesus Christ.'

2 Thessalonians 1:12

JESUS IN THESSALONIANS

Jesus is the Son who is coming from heaven to gather his people and bring a new creation.

QUICK READ

1 Thessalonians 1 – the Faith and Spiritual Experience of the Thessalonians
1 Thessalonians 4:13–18 – the Return of the Lord
2 Thessalonians 2:1–12 – the Man of Lawlessness
2 Thessalonians 3:6–15 – Don't Be Idle

1 and 2 Timothy

The letters to Timothy are deeply pastoral and appreciative of his ministry, encouraging him and teaching about Christian leadership. They are also concerned with guarding the apostolic faith against errors.

Leadership

First Timothy 3 contains instructions for church leadership and service. There is no clear blueprint for the type of church structures that we should have in the Bible – they seem to be varied and flexible in the early church – but there is a clear sense of authority held by the apostles. Gradually the offices described in the New Testament were given the titles of bishop, priest and deacon in the early centuries of the church.

Teaching

Paul returns to the problem of false teaching time and again in these two letters. What exactly was going on in this time and place we do not know; most of his problems encountered elsewhere were with the Judaizers, who were trying to make Gentiles Jews as well as Christians. We seem to be dealing with myths and speculations much more here, which might have come from esoteric Jewish groups with mystical and symbolic ideas or from an early form of Gnosticism. The latter developed endless lists of angelic beings and special codes for reading the Scriptures, as well as new stories of its own about the creation and redemption of the world. They tried to fit Jesus into their system, but they had to radically change him in the process! (See 1 Timothy 1:3–7; 4:1–7.)

The Deposit

Paul tells Timothy to guard the 'deposit' that was entrusted to him (2 Timothy 1:14). The New Testament developed an idea of a rule of faith, a deposit handed down by the apostles. They did not have a completed New Testament for a time, and the church creeds came much later. There was an orally agreed body of teachings that tested a person's doctrine. This was concerned with Jesus really having come in the flesh, really having died and risen again, and with the Holy Spirit's grace and power coming upon the believer. Some were denying that Jesus had real flesh – much Greek thinking downplayed matter and could not conceive of the divine being intimately linked to it. Some denied that he had really died – perhaps he had just appeared to do so. Some denied the resurrection except as an ongoing inner enlightenment.

Confessions of Faith

Though there were no creeds as such, there are signs of various confessions of faith, perhaps sung as hymns to aid memory. First Timothy has two, a saying and a hymn, in 1:15 and 3:16, respectively, which Paul quotes. Second Timothy has a hymn in 2:11–13. These are obviously very early Christian doctrine, and are partly about trust and faithfulness, but also about the reality of the incarnation, resurrection and the power of the Spirit. Paul had his own, fresh ideas, but he stood very much in a developing tradition of faith which he accepted and handed on.

Shipwreck

Paul mentions two believers in 1 Timothy 1 who have made a 'shipwreck' of their faith – Hymenaeus and Alexander. Christians can go very wrong and lose their way, and Paul says that he has handed them over to Satan so that they will learn their lesson. This idea of 'handing over' in such cases, which can also include exclusion from the church assembly, recurs here and there. Church discipline and rightful authority have to be used to protect not only the flock but also the individuals who have gone astray. Note that with the discipline is the hope that they will turn from their sins in the future. In 2 Timothy 4:14, Paul mentions Alexander the metalworker, who has harmed him, and he hands him over, too, to the Lord's judgment.

Women

Paul teaches male headship in 1 Timothy 2:11–15, appealing to the order of creation with Adam and Eve (Adam was made first, then Eve). He also makes a controversial statement about women keeping silent in meetings and being saved through childbirth. The childbirth comment could be referring to God's curse of the serpent in Genesis 3:15 and the implication that through childbearing salvation would come to humanity (i.e. Jesus).

Many are the debates over headship today! Some see this as culturally conditioned, some as the nature of things. Others point out that the Adam and Eve story can be given a different spin, whereby Eve was an equal to Adam, unlike the animals, and a 'helper' (Genesis 2:18–20). This was a term of strength in Hebrew thought, and not of weakness.

Widows

First Timothy 5:3–16 talks about provision for widows. In a society where the extended family supported the elderly, there was no social security system. Paul exhorts families to look after their widows, but says that a widow who has no support should be looked after by the church. He speaks of a 'list of widows' and this sounds almost like a celibate order. No one under 60 should be admitted – the younger women will probably wish to remarry – and they must be of good repute. It is possible that the roots of celibate religious orders of nuns had its beginning in this form of provision and personal dedication to the gospel.

KEY VERSES

1 TIMOTHY

'For there is one God and one mediator between God and men, the man Christ Jesus, who gave himself as a ransom for all men...'

1 Timothy 2:5–6

2 TIMOTHY

'Guard the good deposit that was entrusted to you – guard it with the help of the Holy Spirit who lives in us.'

2 Timothy 1:14

JESUS IN TIMOTHY

Jesus was truly incarnate, appearing in bodily form, and he died for our sins

and rose again. He calls us to be faithful to him. 'He appeared in a body, was vindicated by the Spirit, was seen by angels… was taken up in glory.'
1 Timothy 3:16

QUICK READ

1 Timothy 1:3–11 – the Dangers of False Teaching
1 Timothy 3 – Leadership in the Church
1 Timothy 5:3–16 – Widows
2 Timothy 1 – the Deposit of Faith
2 Timothy 2:8–13 – Paul's Gospel

Titus

The letter to Titus is brief and summarizes some of the points found in the letters to Timothy.

Leadership

Paul gives his criteria for leadership in Titus 1:5–9 and instructs Titus to appoint elders in every town. He then goes on to talk about the qualities of the overseer.

Teaching

Paul warns against false doctrine and touches on the Jewish problem specifically with disputes over the Law. He also mentions myths and genealogies as in Timothy, and we are not sure what this was all about. It might have been an early form of esoteric speculation that developed into the later heresy of Gnosticism.

Live Right, but by Grace

Paul presents a Christian code of holy living in Titus 2 and 3, but he is quick to remind the reader that this must be by grace and not our own efforts. Referring to Jesus, Paul says, 'he saved us, not because of righteous things we had done, but because of his mercy… through the washing of rebirth and renewal by the Holy Spirit' (Titus 3:5).

KEY VERSES

'But when the kindness and love of God our Saviour appeared, he saved us, not because of righteous things we had done, but because of his mercy. He saved us through the washing of rebirth and renewal by the Holy Spirit, whom he poured out on us generously through Jesus Christ our Saviour…' (Titus 3:4–6)

JESUS IN TITUS

Jesus gave himself for us in love and mercy, to wash us and allow the Spirit to be poured out upon us.

QUICK READ

Titus 1:5–9 – Qualifications for Leadership

Philemon

Philemon is one of the shortest letters in the New Testament. It is concerned with merciful treatment for a runaway slave.

Onesimus

Onesimus is a runaway slave who has been imprisoned with and converted by Paul. Paul describes himself as being the slave's spiritual father and thankful that they have met. Onesimus has been a great help to Paul while he has been in prison. Paul writes to Onesimus's master, Philemon, saying he is sending Onesimus back to Philemon and appealing to Philemon for mercy. A master was free, under Roman law, to beat and even kill a runaway slave. Philemon is a Christian brother, and so, too, now, is Onesimus. He is returning no longer as just a slave, but as something far more, a 'dear brother'.

The message of this letter is very simple: it puts the love of Christ into practice. Paul might have accepted slavery as a given in his society, but he helped the Christians to transform it from within. There should be mercy and loyalty together, for as Christian brothers both master and slave were equal before God.

 Later slave traders who claimed it was their right to keep and mistreat slaves were flying in the face of the gospel. Thankfully, some had the courage to abolish this altogether when the time was ripe.

KEY VERSES

'Perhaps the reason he was separated from you for a little while was that you might have him back for good – no longer as a slave, but better than a slave, as a dear brother.'

Philemon verses 15–16

JESUS IN PHILEMON

Jesus is about love, mercy and forgiveness.

QUICK READ

It's so short, just read it all!

Hebrews

The letter to the Hebrews is of anonymous authorship, though it could be by one of Paul's companions or disciples as it shares some of his ideas. It concerns the Jews and the relationship of the new covenant to the old.

Greater Than the Angels

Hebrews 1 proclaims Jesus as the 'Son' who was in existence from the beginning and who is greater than all the angels. The opening description in Hebrews 1:3 uses some imagery that is ascribed to Wisdom in Jewish writings. Later 'Son' imagery is also royal, for it proclaims Jesus as king and messiah.

It is possible that some were speculating about ranks of angels as intermediaries between God and the material world, and trying to fit Jesus into this some way down the ladder. The author will have none of this.

Brothers, Sons and Children

Hebrews 2 uses Psalm 8 to celebrate the incarnation, wherein Jesus was made a 'little lower than the angels' for a time, but then was raised up way above them. His desire was to 'bring many sons to glory', to redeem humankind and to open the way for people to know the Father. The writer again uses Psalms (22) to declare that Jesus' incarnation made him a 'brother' to the human race, and uses Isaiah to show that Jesus' desire is to see many spiritual children born, quoting, 'Here am I and the children God has given me' (Isaiah 8:18).

Greater Than Moses

In Hebrews 3:1–6, Moses, the great Lawgiver of the Jews, is made subservient to Jesus. Jesus was the builder of the house; Moses was the housekeeper. Moses was a servant;

 Jesus was a son. In Roman law, the son inherited and had all the privileges.

Rest

Hebrews 3:7 – 4:11 teaches about the 'rest' of God. This is a novel and original idea in the New Testament and has several angles here. First of all, the 'rest' was the sabbath, when God finished creation. Then the 'rest' was the homeland to abide in that was promised to the Hebrews in the wilderness. Finally, it is a state of grace and forgiveness to live in with God. Jesus has brought a deeper, eternal and spiritual rest for our souls. It is a rest from our own efforts and works and a trust in the mercy and grace of God. This is possible through the sacrifice made on the cross.

The Living Word

Hebrews 4:12–13 teaches that God's word is a living power that will penetrate a potential believer's defences. It is like the Roman *gladius*, the short, stabbing, two-edged sword that could penetrate enemy armour easily. The 'dividing' of soul and spirit suggests that there is a clarity and an insight that goes straight to the heart of the matter when God speaks to us. A thousand human words will fall on deaf ears; one word from God and we listen!

The High Priest

Hebrews 4:14 – 8:13 speaks of Jesus as our high priest. The high priest was a key figure for the Jews. He represented them before God in the Temple at certain points, making offerings and praying for atonement and forgiveness. Only he was allowed to enter the Holy Place, the most sacred area of the Temple where the ark was kept. He had to be called; he could not appoint himself. He was imperfect, he made offerings for himself and they had to be repeated annually.

Jesus is a spiritual high priest who is perfect and whose offering was perfect. It can never be repeated, nor does it need to be. It was once and for all.

Melchizedek

This enigmatic figure is appealed to so that Jesus' high priesthood can be validated. Jesus was not of the line of Levi, and Jewish high priests had to be of that lineage. Jesus is of a different order, a different lineage.

Melchizedek was an ancient king of Jerusalem who appears in Genesis 14 in the story of Abraham. We are told next to nothing about him. Abraham makes offerings to him of a tenth of his produce. In Hebrew thought, Levi was present in Abraham's genes, and so, by proxy, Levi made offerings to him, too. That made Melchizedek greater than Levi.

Hebrews 7:1–3 toys with the idea that we are told nothing about Melchizedek. He just appears and disappears in the story of Abraham. The author reads into this figure a type of Christ, one who had no beginning and no end. Thus his high priesthood is greater, as it is eternal. This might sound like clever poetics, but there is a deeper link. The author also quotes Psalm 110, which declares, 'You are a priest for ever, in the order of Melchizedek.' This is the only other mention of him in the Old Testament.

Scholars feel that this Psalm was a royal Psalm, and might have been part of a coronation ceremony. King David captured Jerusalem and made it his capital; when the Israelite kings became established there, they might have taken over some of the older Jerusalem rituals. Melchizedek seems to have combined the roles of priest and king, something which Jewish kings were forbidden to do (and a misdeed that got Saul into trouble). Yet, Zechariah seems to have prophesied that the messiah would be priestly and royal (Zechariah 6:9–13), which made the Jews think that there might be two separate messianic figures to come. In fact, so the author of Hebrews says, Jesus had fulfilled a much earlier role, that of Melchizedek, who was both a king and a priest together. He had gone back before the Law.

Blood and Sacrifice

Hebrews 9:11–15 describes how Jesus made atonement through his blood in the heavens and not just in an earthly sanctuary that was a shadow of the eternal dwelling place of God. By the unique power of this eternal offering, he became the mediator of a new covenant. Hebrews 10:1–14 explains why his offering was perfect and cannot be repeated. Christians live in the power and covering shadow of that offering. This gives them confidence to enter into God's presence by 'a new and living way' (Hebrews 10:20a). The old Holy Place, God's dwelling on earth, had a dividing curtain; Jesus has removed this spiritually and Christians are free to approach.

Faith

Hebrews 11 is a chronicle of the heroes of faith. The author wants to encourage his readers to stand firm in the face of opposition. Faith is defined here as something that can be sure and certain, even though we have no proof that can be seen. Faith in the New Testament is not a blind leap in the dark, but confidence and trust in the Holy Spirit.

Hebrews 12:1–3 urges us to run the race of faith, fixing our eyes on Jesus and not on the problems around us. The heroes of the past, the saints of the Old Testament are a 'great cloud of witnesses' rooting for us as they live with God today. Their stories encourage and inspire.

Discipline

Hebrews 12:4–13 teaches that hardship can school us, refining faith and bringing discipline. A true father will discipline a son, and God will guide us with a loving (and sometimes firm) hand.

KEY VERSES

'Therefore, brothers, since we have confidence to enter the Most Holy Place by the blood of Jesus, by a new and living way… let us draw near to God with a sincere heart in full assurance of faith…'

Hebrews 10:19–22

JESUS IN HEBREWS

Jesus is the eternal Son, greater than the angels, greater than Moses, who is our high priest.

QUICK READ

Hebrews 1 – the Son and the Angels
Hebrews 2:5–18 – Jesus as Brother and Gathering Children
Hebrews 4:1–11 – Rest for the People of God
Hebrews 4:12–13 – the Living and Active Word of God
Hebrews 4:14 – 5:10 – Jesus the High Priest and Melchizedek
Hebrews 10:1–18 – Jesus' Sacrifice Once for All
Hebrews 11 – Heroes of Faith

James

The letter of James is Hebrew in thought and style, speaking of morality and lifestyle.

Which James?

James was Jesus' brother and the leader of the church in Jerusalem when Peter and John moved away on their missions and James the apostle was martyred. (There are debates about what 'brother' means, with some taking this as literal, some as stepbrother or cousin, but he was a close relation of Jesus.)

Wisdom and Trials

In the first chapter, James urges us to ask God for wisdom when we lack it, and not to be of two minds about serving him. Temptations do not come from God, but he will give us the strength to stand against them. James is concerned with spiritual integrity, urging us to act on the word and not to hear it only. He contrasts earthly and heavenly wisdom in James 3:13–18, showing how one causes pride and one is honest, open to correction and gentle.

High and Low

In chapter 2, James has no time for human pride and status in worship. Rich and poor should mix and there should be no favourites. In James 4:1–12 he adds to this theme, stating that God resists the proud but is close to the humble (as in the principle of Mary's song, the Magnificat).

Works

James appeals to the value of good works and seems to contradict Paul's teaching about justification by faith in James

2:14–26. He even uses the example of Abraham, stressing that it was his obedience and not his faith alone that made him righteous. This so upset the reformer Martin Luther that he argued that this letter should not be in scripture, calling it an 'epistle of straw'!

It depends upon the interpretation, though. Perhaps James was reacting to an exaggerated use of Paul's ideas by some of his followers. Maybe James was opposed to Paul himself, as we note that when Paul visited Jerusalem towards the end of his life, James did not welcome him. This shows the power of malicious gossip and misrepresentation that can happen between Christians.

Paul did not teach that intellectual assent alone was salvific; one had to act, to do, to commit oneself. Faith is an active, trusting thing. James recognizes that real faith, living faith, must have actions that follow. Faith without works is dead. In a nutshell, real, saving faith will result in actions, as fruit from a tree.

The Tongue

The power of the tongue, as in the power of our words to hurt or heal, is the subject of James 3:1–12. Its power is akin to a ship's rudder, which is a small thing that steers the whole vessel. We should not praise God and curse men at the same time.

Healing and Confession

In James 5:13–20 he teaches that a sick person should be brought to the elders, who will pray over him or her and anoint with holy oil. The use of olive oil for medicinal and cosmetic purposes in ancient times was widespread, and the early church obviously blessed such oil and used it as a symbol of God's Holy Spirit. This practice carried on in the Roman Catholic, Orthodox and Anglican Churches, but it is being rediscovered by many Free and New Churches in the charismatic movement.

The readers are urged to confess their sins to one another (James 5:16) and not just privately, to God. There is no doubt that sometimes we need that extra support. The practice of confession to an elder (or priest) in some churches arose partly from this.

KEY VERSE

'But the wisdom that comes from heaven is first of all pure; then peace – loving, considerate, submissive, full of mercy and good fruit, impartial and sincere.'

James 3:17

JESUS IN JAMES

Jesus is only mentioned by name twice in this letter.

QUICK READ

James 1:2–8, 3:13–17 – Wisdom from God

James 1:19–27 – Be Doers of the Word

James 2:1–13, 4:1–12 – Be Humble, Not Proud

James 5:13–20 – Prayer for the Sick and Confessing Sins

1 and 2 Peter

Peter's letters cover various issues, speaking of new birth, the priesthood of all believers, suffering, false teaching and the coming of the Lord.

New Birth

Peter's letters are the only other use of the term 'born again' or 'new birth' in the New Testament apart from Jesus speaking to Nicodemus in John 3. Many other ideas and images are used as well to speak of conversion and coming to faith. First Peter 1:3, 1:23 and 2:2 use the new birth image.

All Are Priests

First Peter 2:4–10 describes Christians as a chosen people, a holy nation and a royal priesthood. Each believer is a priest before God, with equal access to his presence and in need of no mediator but Jesus. (The title 'priest' for Christian leaders can be misleading, but it is really a shortened form of the Greek word *presbyter*, meaning 'elder'. Only some are called to be leaders and ordained; all stand as priests before God.)

Trials and Suffering

First Peter 1:6–9 speaks of the refining of our faith through trials, just as gold is purified in the fire. First Peter 3:8–17 speaks of suffering for righteousness' sake – that is, when one does not deserve it. This brings blessing, and Jesus trod the same path.

Preaching to the Dead?

In 1 Peter 3:18–20 and 4:6 Jesus is said to have preached to the spirits of the dead, including those who died in the Flood. The power of his forgiveness and resurrection is seen to extend beyond this world. These passages cause lively debates. Was this just a special grace for those in the Flood, or was it for all of those who came before his life on earth? Is it an ongoing, eternal event? Is the grave too late, or is there a chance for the dead to hear the gospel? Some feel that this would give a fair chance to followers of other religions without infringing upon Jesus' statement that no one comes to God except through him.

False Teachers

Second Peter 2 warns against those who depart from the faith and 2 Peter 1:16 pours scorn on cleverly devised myths, saying that the gospel is based upon real events of which Peter was an eyewitness. False teachers who deny the important and central tenets of the faith are like 'springs without water' or 'mists driven by a storm' – they lack life and substance. How true this is today for scholars and ministers who deny the divinity of Christ, the resurrection or the very existence of God!

The Day of the Lord

Second Peter 3 contains teaching about the return of Jesus. No matter how long it seems to be delayed (and the first Christians thought it was literally around the corner), it will happen. The world is in God's hands. Peter quotes Psalm 90:4, saying a thousand days are as a single day to the Lord. His time scheme is not ours.

Prophets

Both of Peter's letters speak of the prophets of the past and of how they pointed towards Jesus, not always realizing what they were saying. First Peter 1:10–12 has them serving not themselves but the Christian believer, who has now entered into what was promised. Peter adds the enigmatic phrase, 'Even angels long to look into these things.' (Paul also speaks of the mystery of the faith, and how it was hidden in the past – see Ephesians 3:8–10.) Second Peter 1:19–21 returns to this theme, pointing out the role of the Spirit in prophecy and how we need the Spirit to interpret it today.

KEY VERSES

I PETER

'In his great mercy he has given us new birth into a living hope through the resurrection of Jesus Christ from the dead, and into an inheritance that can never perish, spoil or fade – kept in heaven for you…'

I Peter 1:3b–4

2 PETER

'For prophecy never had its origin in the will of man, but men spoke from God as they were carried along by the Holy Spirit.'

2 Peter 1:21

JESUS IN PETER

Jesus gives new birth and new hope. He was truly incarnate and truly risen, and was foretold by the prophets.

QUICK READ

1 Peter 1:3–12 – Our Great Salvation and Hope

1 Peter 2:4–10 – a Royal Priesthood

1 Peter 3:18–20; 4:6 – Preaching to the Spirits of the Dead

2 Peter 1:12–21 – the Prophets

2 Peter 2 – False Teachers

2 Peter 3 – the Day of the Lord

The Letters of John

The second and third of the three letters of John are very short indeed, but his first letter speaks more fully of Jesus coming in the flesh, of forgiveness and of love.

Handling the Word of Life

First John 1:1–4 declares that what is being preached is not a fairy tale but solid history – the writer claims to have been an eyewitness. (Traditionally he is thought to be the apostle John.)

The Light

We are exhorted to 'walk in the light' as there is no darkness in God. If we sin, the sacrifice of Jesus on the cross can still cleanse and forgive us (see 1 John 1:7–10). This is important, for soon after this letter was written some wondered if sin committed after baptism could ever be forgiven. John states that if we keep in fellowship with Jesus and one another, then we will be constantly purified of sin by the blood of Jesus. The blood is seen as an ongoing spiritual power here, as well as something that was offered in real history once for all.

Antichrists

John warns against false teachers and the spirit of antichrist which denies that Jesus was really in the flesh. John is speaking here against a heresy known as Docetism, which taught that Jesus only appeared to be human, for matter was inferior and beneath the dignity of God (see 1 John 2:18–26; 4:1–6). By 'antichrist' here, John does not mean a specific individual but a movement and any false teacher who denies the Lordship of Jesus.

The Anointing Within

John teaches that those who have the Spirit have an inner anointing or discernment to test what is of God and what is not (see 1 John 2:20–21; 5:10). We can discern what is of the Spirit and what is of a false spirit; for the Spirit-filled believer, some things are obviously right and some are not. This is beyond reason, often, and is a strong intuition.

Love

John urges his readers to love one another. God is love, and anyone who hates his brother cannot really love God. Tradition has it that as an old man, John's last sermon was simply 'Love one another.'

2 and 3 John

Second John emphasizes teaching about love. This is not really anything new but it has always been taught. This letter also reiterates the danger of denying that Jesus came in the flesh – and still comes, by his Spirit, into us.

Third John is a personal message to his friend Gaius and a warning about a gossiping individual called Diotrephes.

KEY VERSE

'This is the message we have heard from him and declare to you: God is light; in him there is no darkness at all.'

1 John 1:5

JESUS IN JOHN'S LETTERS

Jesus is the love of God made flesh, a real incarnated being, and our ongoing saviour when we sin.

QUICK READ

1 John 1:1–4 – Real Events

1 John 1:5–10 – Walking in the Light and the Blood of Christ

1 John 2:18–27; 4:1–6 – False Teaching, Antichrists and Our Inner Anointing

1 John 4:7–21 – the Love of God and Our Need to Love

Jude

Jude's short letter warns against false teaching, using many examples from the Old Testament, as befitting a Jewish Christian and the brother of the Lord.

Libertines

The false teachers whom Jude attacks are saying that sexual morality does not matter. They were presumably some of the early Gnostics, or a group akin to them, who denied that the flesh mattered. One could do what one wanted with one's body so long as one's spirit was on the right track! Lists of Old Testament figures and incidents are used to condemn them, such as the judgment on the people of Sodom and Gomorrah.

Interestingly, Jude quotes from the book of Enoch (Jude verse 14). This is not in the Hebrew Old Testament or the Apocryphal books that the Greek Old Testament included. It was another Jewish writing, probably from the 1st century BC, which had great popularity and influence. Was Jude treating it as scripture or just a wise writing? We are not sure, but we must not forget that the canon of scripture was not fixed at this time.

Rebuke

There is a striking passage about even angels not slandering and cursing demons, citing an occasion when the archangel Michael simply asked the Lord to rebuke Satan (verse 9). Apparently the false teachers would go around cursing angelic beings, trying to show their superiority over them. These people were heretics, but today's Christians involved in prayers about spiritual warfare should take note. Hand the matter over to God, be courteous but firm and do not tackle forces head-on that we are not meant to deal with.

Holy Spirit

Jude exhorts us to 'pray in the Holy Spirit', a simple phrase but a deep truth. Paul speaks of the Spirit praying within us (Romans 8:26–27).

KEY VERSE

'To those who have been called, who are loved by God the Father and kept by Jesus Christ.'

Jude verse 1b

JESUS IN JUDE

He is Lord, saviour, mercy and one who is able to keep us from falling.

QUICK READ

It's not too long; read the whole thing.

Revelation

The book of Revelation deals with symbolic visions and promises about the coming Kingdom of God and the return of Christ.

Who?

The author of Revelation is traditionally 'St John the Divine', or the apostle John. Some scholars wonder if this is a different John. Whoever it was, he was in exile on the Greek island of Patmos for his faith. The book opens with a shattering vision of the risen Jesus (Revelation 1:12–18) which makes John fall down as though dead – he is in the presence of the Holy One. Jesus did continue to speak and teach after his resurrection and some of his recorded words come through visions.

Some parts of the book are obscure and hard to understand; its codes and symbols have exercised many imaginations, and buckets of ink have been used to write various ideas and doctrines. Its general themes are clear, though, and deal with faith, trials, victory and the triumph of Christ over evil. The symbol of the Beast rang true for Christians suffering at the hands of Rome, but other rulers can fill those shoes all too easily in today's world! Avoid attempts to codify this book and present exact charts of the end times, for it uses symbols and not literal facts. Jesus himself warned his disciples, 'It is not for you to know the times or dates the Father has set by his own authority…' (Acts 1:7).

To the Seven Churches

The risen Lord gives John a series of messages for seven churches – the churches being symbolized by the seven golden lampstands seen in John's vision (see Revelation 2–3):

- ❑ Ephesus – this church has lost its first love for Jesus; things are sincere but probably becoming routine.

- ❑ Smyrna – they will suffer but will receive their reward. They are faithful.

- ❑ Pergamum – though most are faithful, some are listening to false teachers (it is not certain who the Nicolaitans were).

❑ Thyatira – some are tolerating a lying, devious spiritual influence symbolized by the figure of Jezebel, after the idolatrous Old Testament queen.

❑ Sardis – they are urged to stay faithful like a few among them who truly walk with Jesus.

❑ Philadelphia – they will overcome opposition if they remain faithful. Jesus reveals himself to be the 'key of David' here, meaning that he has all authority.

❑ Laodicea – they are 'lukewarm' and need to repent. If they will, Jesus will enter and eat with them.

Heavenly Visions

Revelation chapters 4–11 have John taken up into heaven for a series of transcendent visions full of codes and symbols. He sees 24 elders in white with golden crowns, the awesome angelic beings with six wings and eyes all over them, and a Lamb who alone is worthy to open a sealed scroll. This Lamb, who had been slain, receives the worship of heaven and earth, with all creation singing, 'Worthy is the Lamb, who was slain, to receive power and wealth and wisdom and strength and honour and glory and praise!' (Revelation 5:12).

The Lamb opens a series of seven seals, each symbolizing an action of God and of coming judgment. John sees 144,000 'servants' sealed as saved and precious to God. This is a symbolic and not a literal number, being 12 x 12,000. This is the totality of all human beings who are Christ's throughout history, and the actual number will be far more than 144,000!

When the seventh seal is opened, there is silence in heaven for half an hour. Then judgment is unleashed by seven angelic trumpets. John is met by an angel who orders him to eat a scroll that is handed to him. Once it is in his stomach, he is told to go and prophesy (see Revelation 10).

Women, Dragons and Beasts

Revelation 12 has a symbolic depiction of the church, the incarnation and spiritual warfare. Michael the archangel struggles against Satan and throws him down to earth. Revelation 13 speaks of the Beast who has control of the nations, an antichrist figure. His number is 666, which is three times the Hebrew number for evil. Three times is utter power (think of the Trinity). This man is evil incarnate! Some have worked out that the Roman emperor Nero's name could generate this number, as can others, but the mark of the Beast involves worship of an evil thing; it is a sign of devotion to darkness, just as the 144,000 sealed by the angels are devoted to the light. Speculations about computer chips under the skin forget this; the mark is not technology but a symbol of worship.

Babylon and the Coming King

After various visions of judgment upon the Beast's people, John sees a harlot sitting on a scarlet beast in Revelation 17. She is known as 'Babylon' but symbolizes Rome, 'the great city that rules over the kings of the earth'. Babylon falls as an angel descends and a lament goes up for her.

Revelation 19 has heaven erupting in worship and the King arriving on a white horse, bearing the title 'King of Kings and Lord of Lords'.

Endings...

There is a strange chronology in Revelation 20 about a thousand-year reign of Christ, and then judgment comes upon Satan and he is cast into the lake of fire along with 'death and Hades'. The New Jerusalem follows (Revelation 21), when God dwells with his people, and the River of Life is there for all (Revelation 22). Trees grow along its banks, and their leaves are 'for the healing of the nations'. The book ends with the prayer *Maranatha!* which is Aramaic for 'Come, Lord!'

KEY VERSE

'I am the Alpha and the Omega,' says the Lord God, 'who is, and who was, and who is to come, the Almighty.'

Revelation 1:8

JESUS IN REVELATION

Jesus is the Lamb who was slain, the Alpha and the Omega, the coming King of Kings and Lord of Lords.

QUICK READ

Revelation 1:12–20 – the Vision of the Risen Jesus

Revelation 2–3 – Messages to the Churches

Revelation 4 – Worship in Heaven

Revelation 12 – the Woman, Child, Dragon and Archangel

Revelation 13 – Beasts

Revelation 19 – the Second Coming

Revelation 21 – the New Jerusalem

Revelation 22:1–6 – the River of Life

Miracles and the Bible

The question of miracles both excites and causes pause for thought. What is a 'miracle', or, when is a miracle not a miracle?

Some definitions of a miracle say that it is a wonderful event in which God shows his hand, however subtly. Other definitions stress that there is a supernatural event and that the normal laws of physics or biology are bypassed or temporarily suspended. By the first definition, a converted alcoholic who restores his or her family life is a case of a miracle. Or, again, an earthquake which happens when the Hebrews are attacking Jericho is a happy coincidence – a God-incidence, if you will. There is still something holy and spiritual about these encounters, even though the normal laws of the cosmos are not bypassed.

In paranormal research, there is a maxim that what *can* be explained by natural forces (physical and psychological) should be so explained. Only when these routes are exhausted do we admit that something paranormal or supernatural is going on. This is balanced, common sense. With the Scriptures, scholars take differing views of some of the miracle stories. There are some ultraliberal sceptics, of course, who cannot bring themselves to admit the presence of anything paranormal or supernatural, but a more believing and balanced approach would affirm the following:

❑ Some miracles might be explained by 'happy coincidences' such as the walls of Jericho falling because of an earthquake, or the waters of the Red Sea rolling back because of a strong wind that blew all night. God's hand can still be discerned in the timing of these events.

❑ Some things might be symbolic rather than literal events. Jesus turning water into wine, for example, can be a vivid symbol of bringing new spiritual life into a tired, old system of religion. Others point out that a literal event such as calming a storm can also have a symbolic application, and if Jesus really was God incarnate, then he could have suspended or bypassed the normal laws of nature to perform such a feat.

❑ There are numerous healing miracles in the Bible, especially in the Gospels. Jesus was a healer and a teacher in the earliest sources that we have, and so were some of the apostles. Sceptics may attribute these healings to the power of psychology, but most modern Christians believe in the power of God to heal today. Most acknowledge, however, that why healing happens for some and not for others is a mystery.

❑ That said, some do point out that there are huge gaps in our knowledge of how the mind can affect the body. A hypnotized person can be told that a cold iron bar is red hot, and their skin will blister. A guilt-wracked person can slip into a coma-like state of catatonia. It is possible that at least some of the Gospel cures were healings of the mind and spirit through faith and the alleviation of guilt and psychological anguish in the presence of God through Jesus. Note that in the story of the paralysed man who was lowered through the roof (Mark 2:1–12), Jesus tells him that his sins are forgiven before he tells him to get up and walk.

Lastly, there are other major events such as the virgin birth and the resurrection which cannot be explained away. Some scholars do try to give a degree of symbolic interpretation to these, but this stance is highly debatable. They think that the virgin birth was just a symbolic story to show that Jesus was special, being 'God made man'. They argue that Jesus is alive spiritually but question some of the resurrection stories as being too literal. If Jesus was literally born of a virgin, then we are dealing with a bypassing or a suspension of physical laws. In the resurrection, a body disappeared, was transformed into spiritual energy and made tactile contact with the disciples for a time, according to all the New Testament traditions. People either try to water this down or they embrace the tradition in all its mysterious richness.

To sum up, some miracle stories can be explained as 'happy coincidences or God-incidences' where the miracle is in the timing. Some can be psychological and spiritual, wherein the healing of guilt might free up limbs to walk. Some things cannot be explained except to appeal to a suspension or a bypassing of natural laws.

Believers should at least recognize that where the presence of God is, there will be blessings and new life. When his supernatural presence meets nature, we should be open for all sorts of things to happen.

Further Reading

This pocket guide is a basic introduction to the Bible and its books. If you want to go deeper in your study, then there are numerous commentaries and handbooks that are very useful.

One idea to help you read through the Scriptures is to use a One Year Bible, available in various translations. This gives you sections of the Old Testament and New Testament to read each day. You could use *A Pocket Guide to the Bible* to get some background and then use further resources for more information.

A LITTLE DEEPER...

These resources will help you study in a little more depth. They are readable and highly visual.

- ❑ *The Lion Handbook to the Bible*, by David and Pat Alexander (Lion)
- ❑ *Journey Through the Bible*, by V. Gilbert Bees (Monarch)
- ❑ *The Bible Application Handbook*, by J.I. Packer and Derek Williams (Eagle)
- ❑ *The Bible Guide*, by Andrew Knowles (Lion)

DEEPER STILL...

There are one-volume commentaries on the Bible and single-book commentaries. The one-volume editions can be tilted towards a more academic approach, but have much useful material. They also tend to be expensive. Two excellent ones are:

❑ *The Jerome Bible Commentary*, edited by Raymond E. Brown, Joseph A. Fitzmyer, Roland E. Murphy (Geoffrey Chapman)

❑ *The Oxford Bible Companion*, edited by J. Barton and John Muddiman (Oxford University Press)

❑ *New Bible Commentary*, edited by D.A. Carson, R.T. France, J. Alec Motyer, Gordon J. Wenham (IVP)

Examples of some good, accessible and devotional single-book commentaries are:

❑ *The Tyndale Bible Commentaries* (IVP)

❑ *The Bible Speaks Today* series (IVP)

VERY DEEP!

There are some very seriously academic and thorough commentaries for those who wish to dip into ancient languages and lots of scholarly ideas. Two examples of intelligent but reverent series are:

❑ *The Anchor Bible Commentaries* (Random House)

❑ The *Sacra Pagina* series on the Gospels (Michael Glazier)